DONATION GLICKSMAN

CALIFORNIAN STORIES, 1960S–1970S

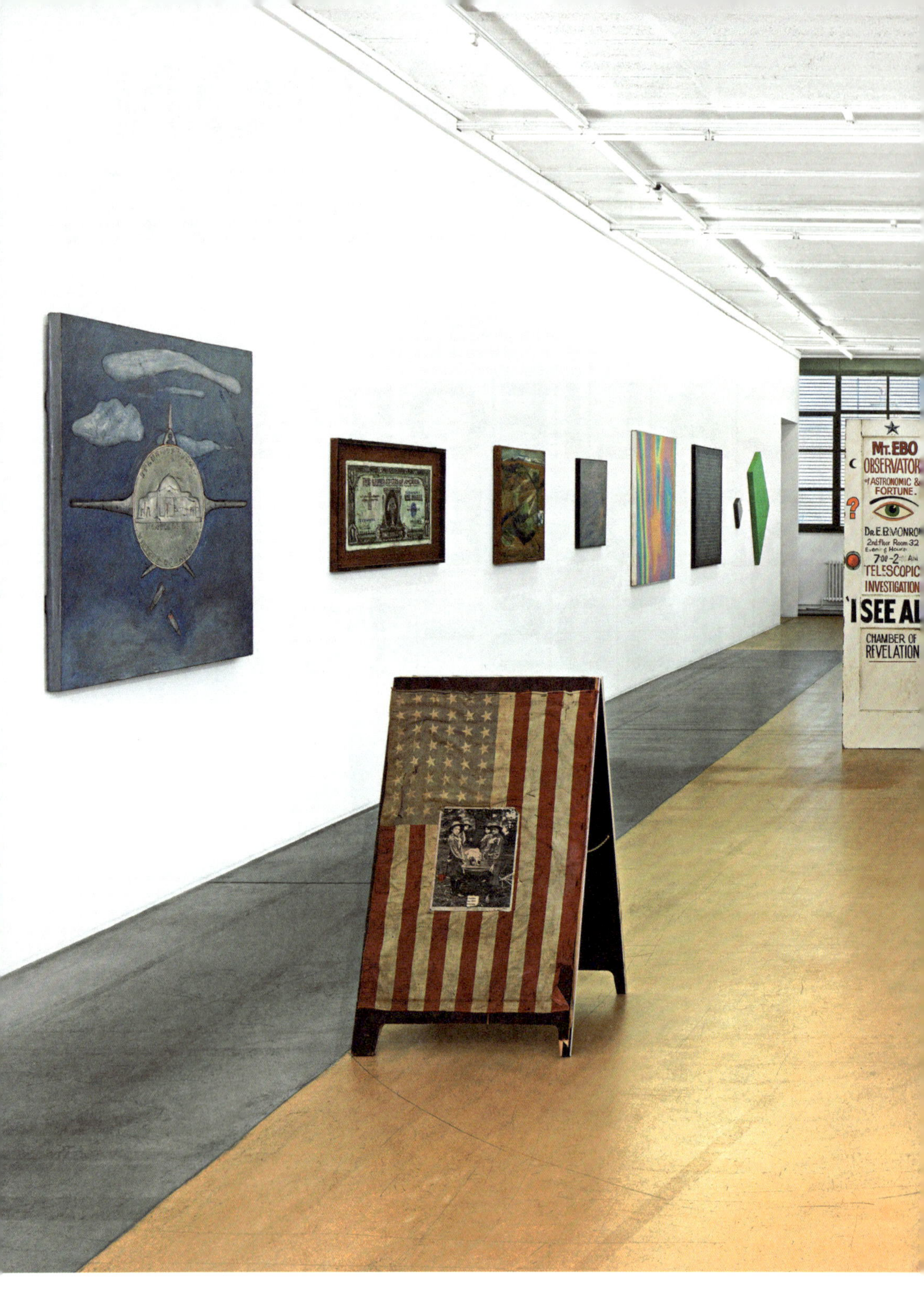
Mt. EBO
OBSERVATORY
of ASTRONOMIC &
FORTUNE.
Dr. E.B. MONRO
2nd floor Room 32
Evening Hours
7:00 - 2:00 AM
TELESCOPIC
INVESTIGATION
'I SEE AL
CHAMBER OF
REVELATION

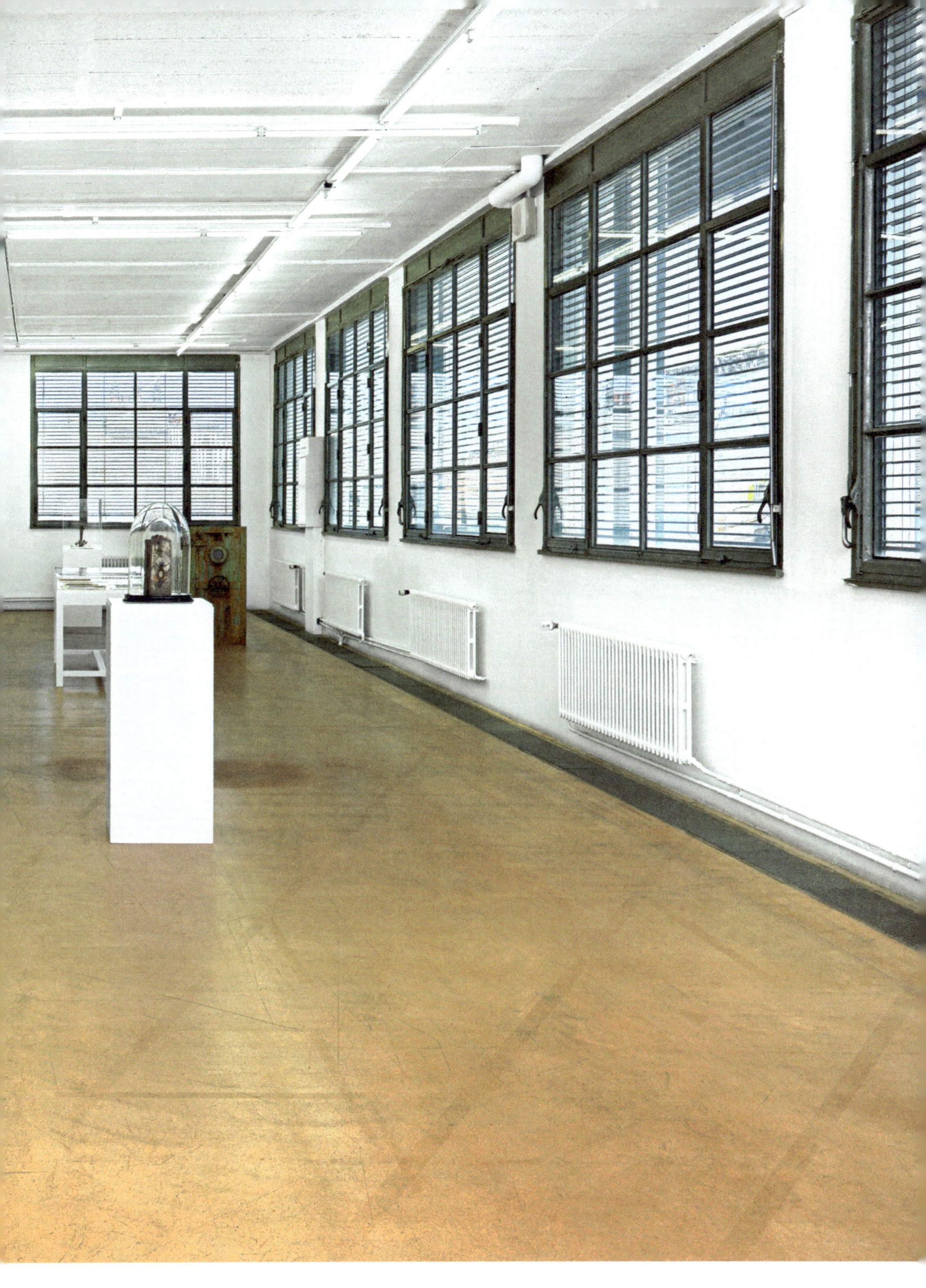

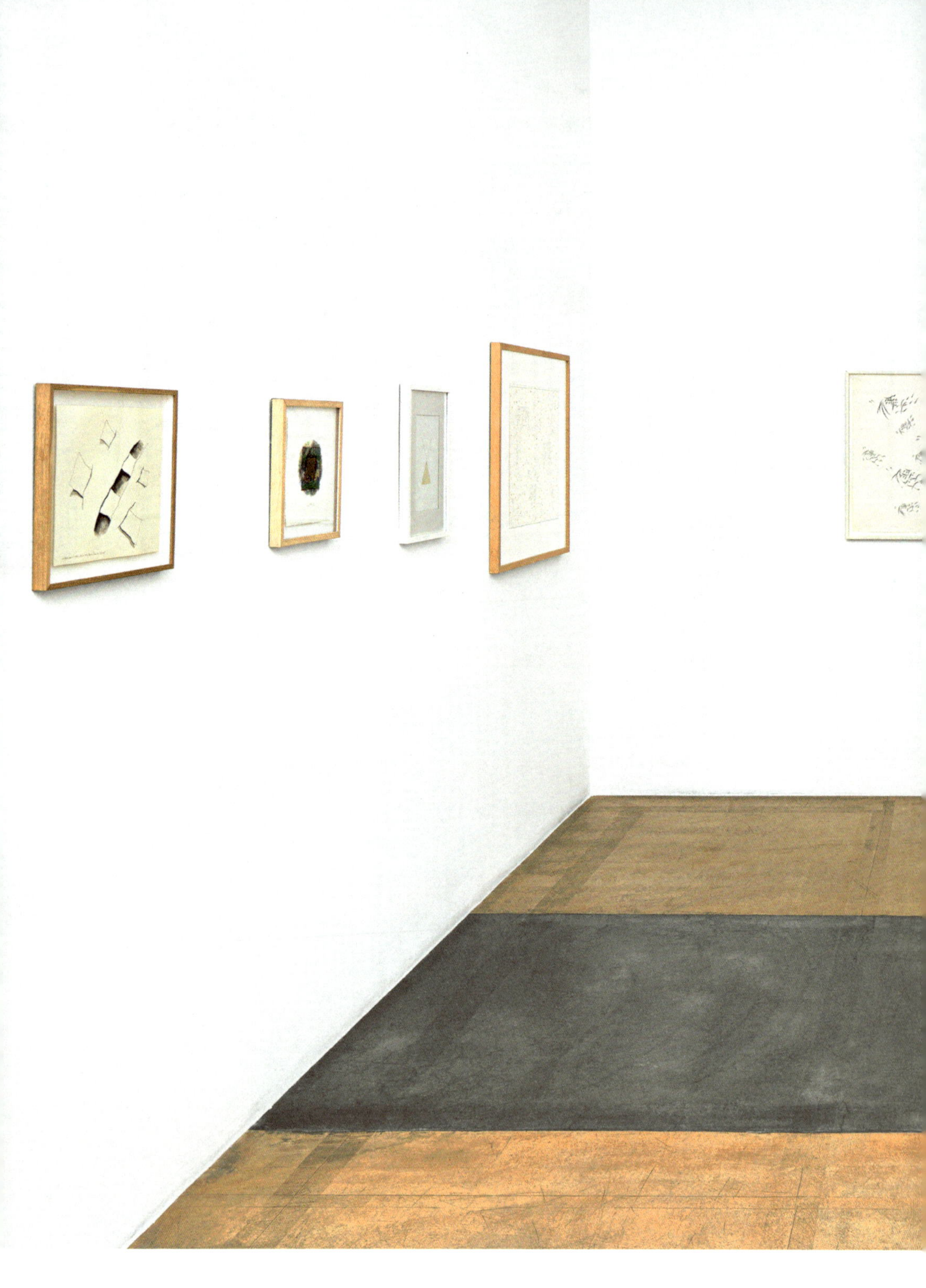

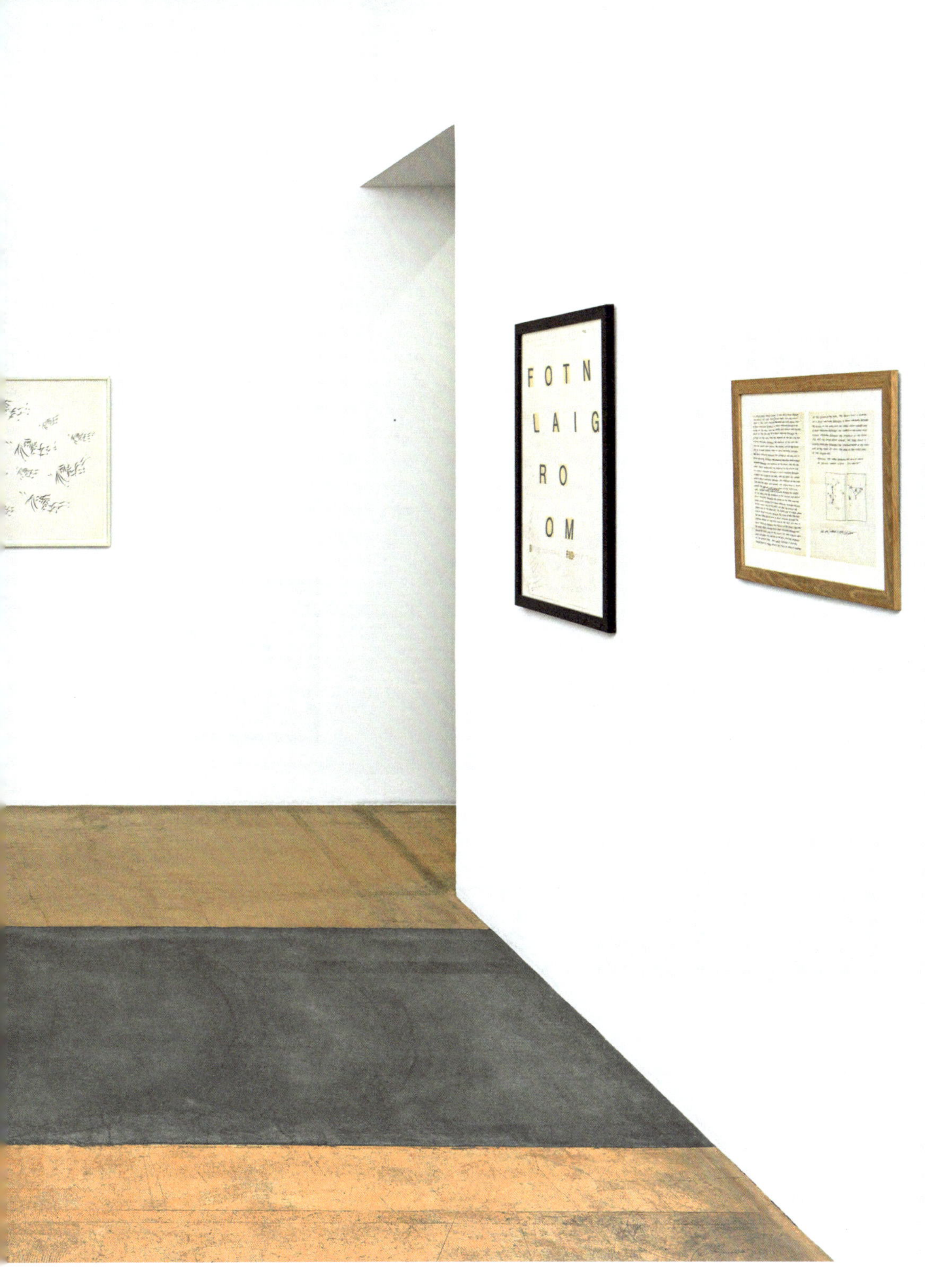

Donation Glicksman, MAMCO, Geneva 2024

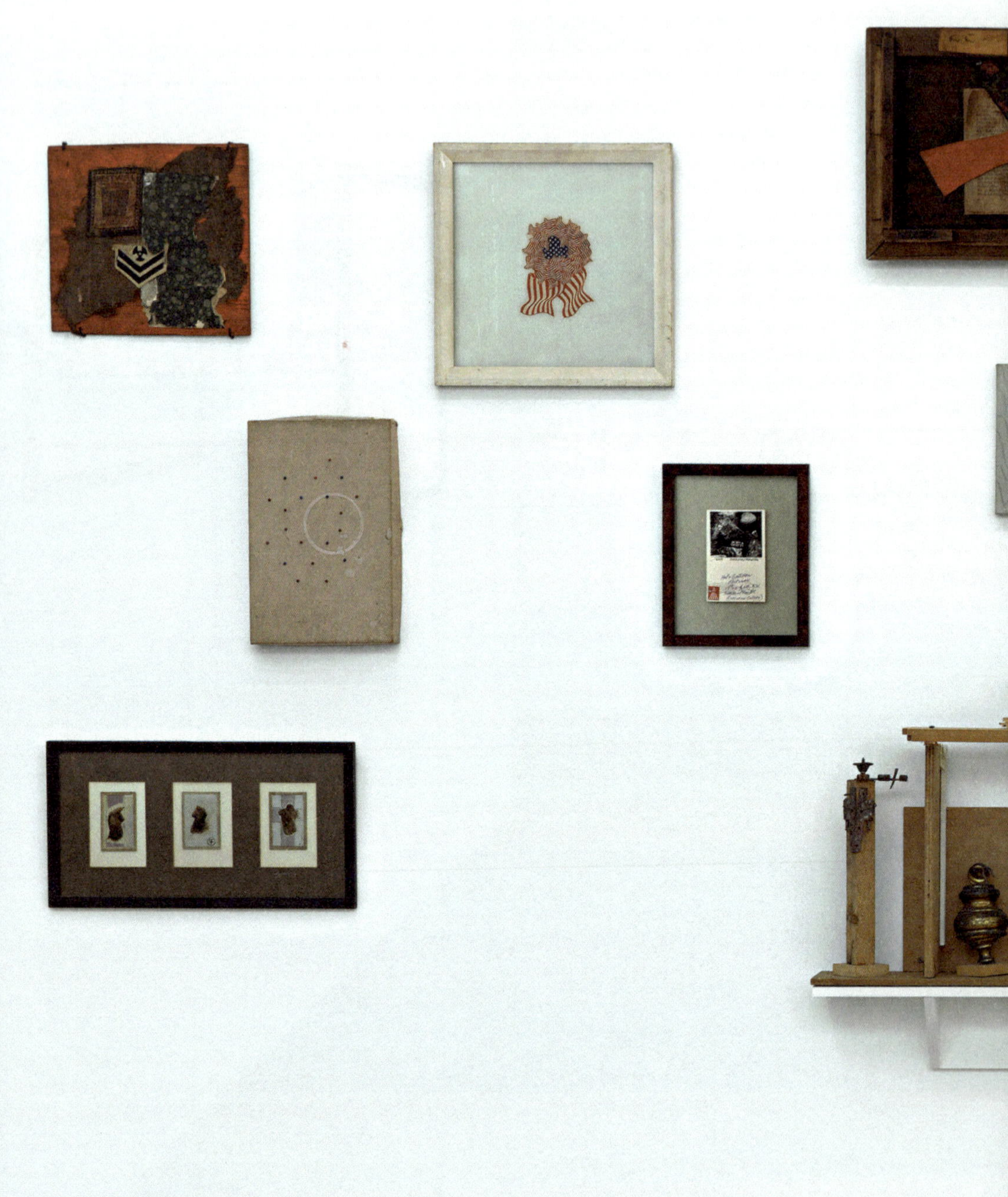

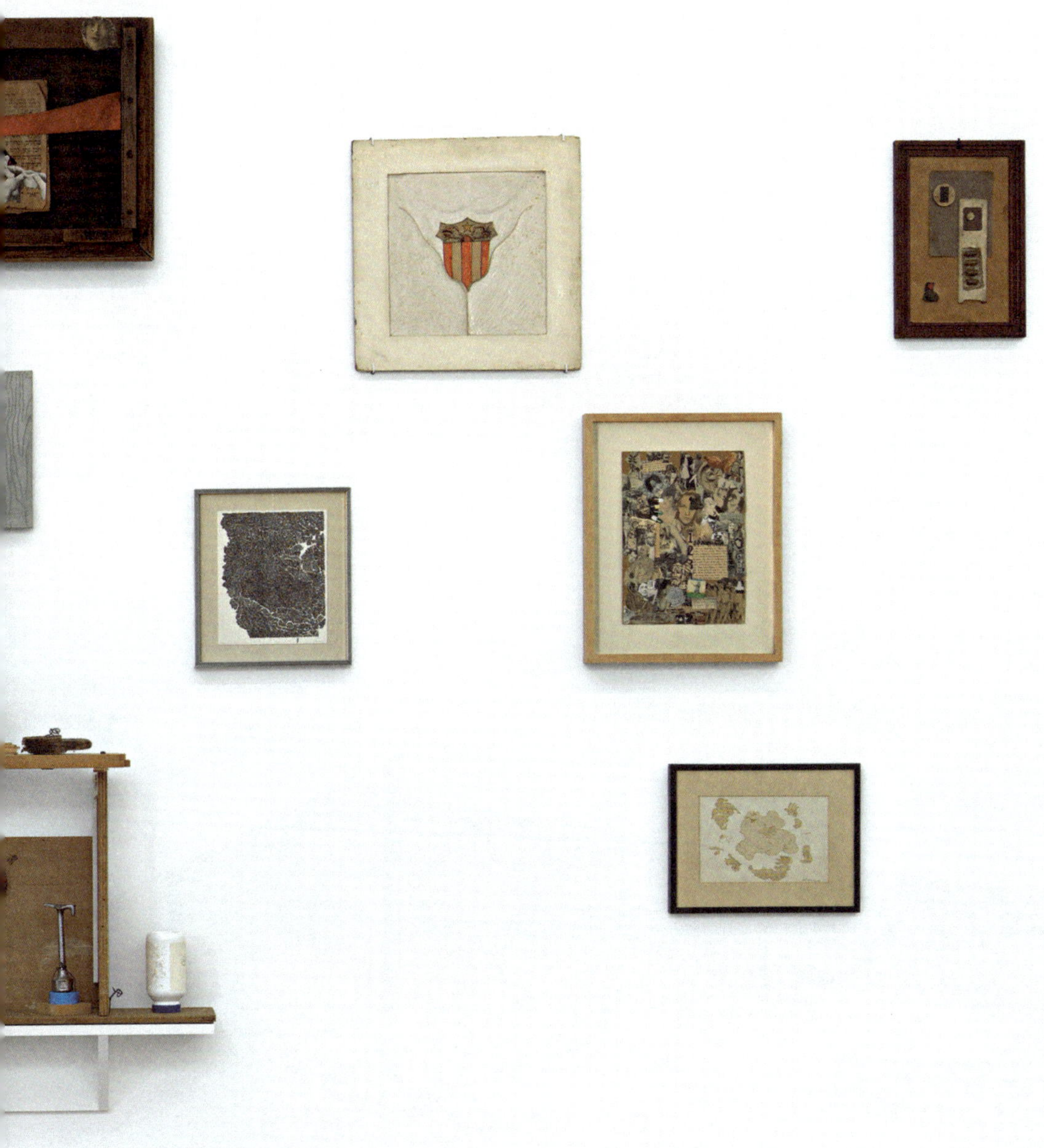

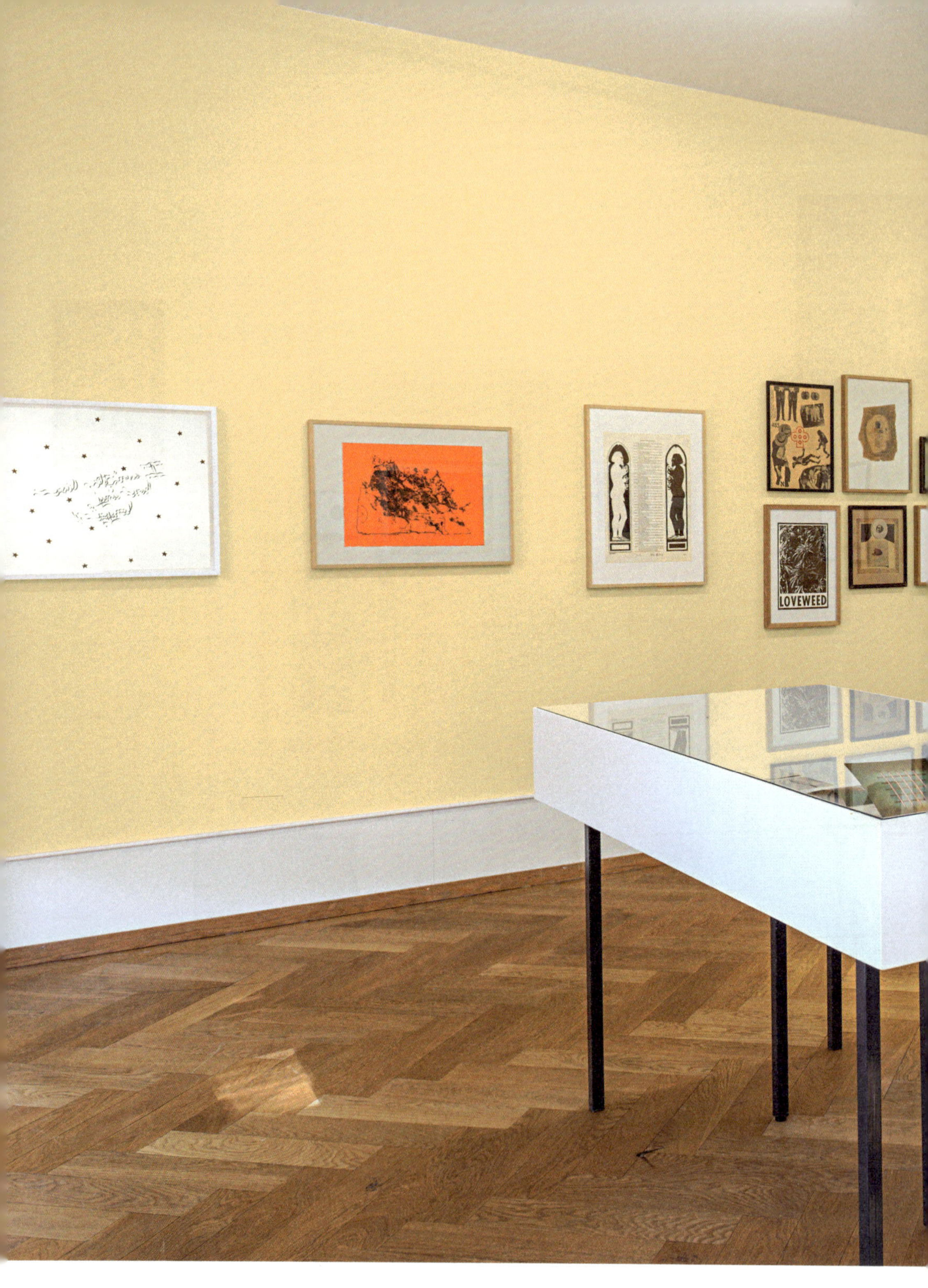

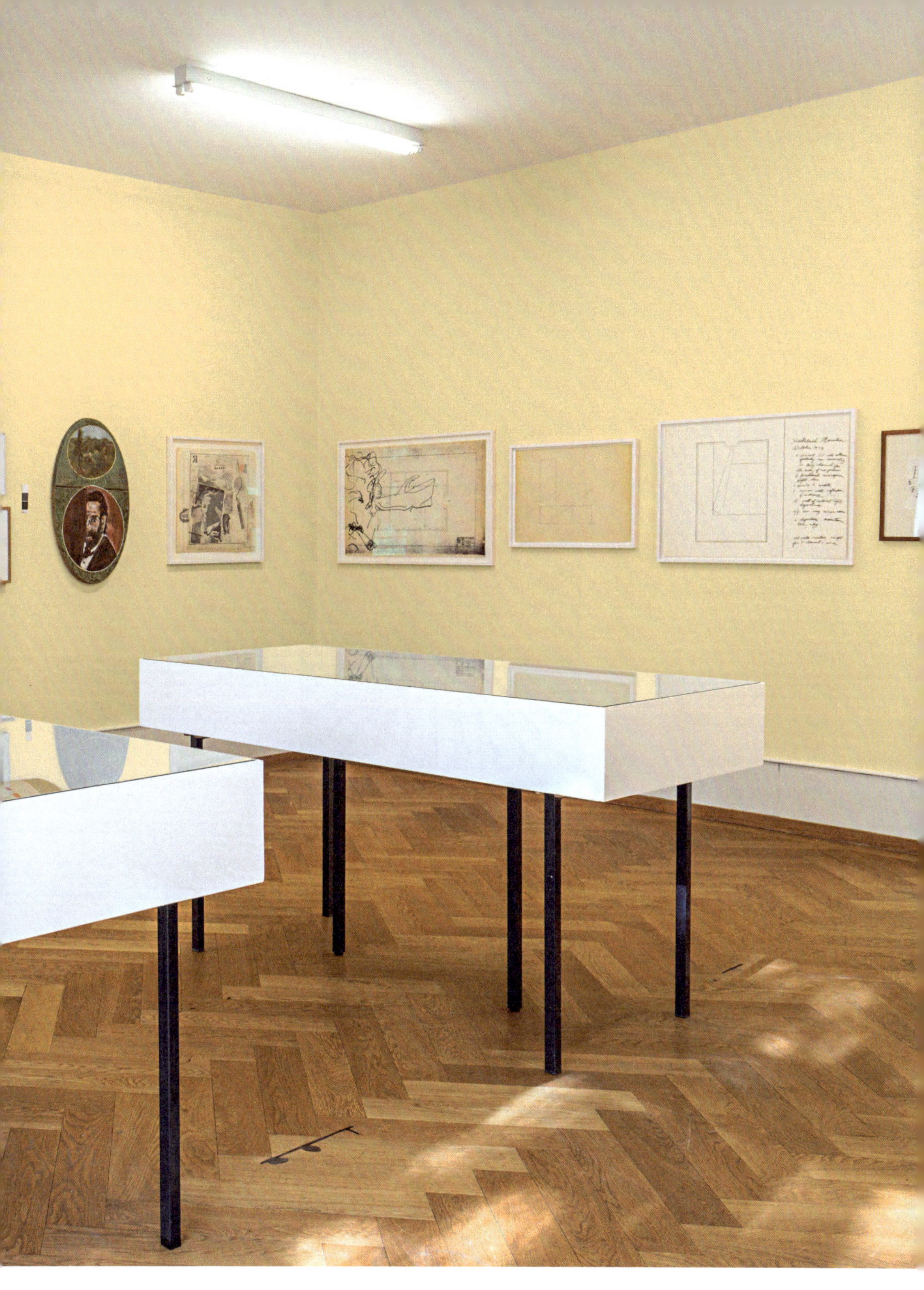

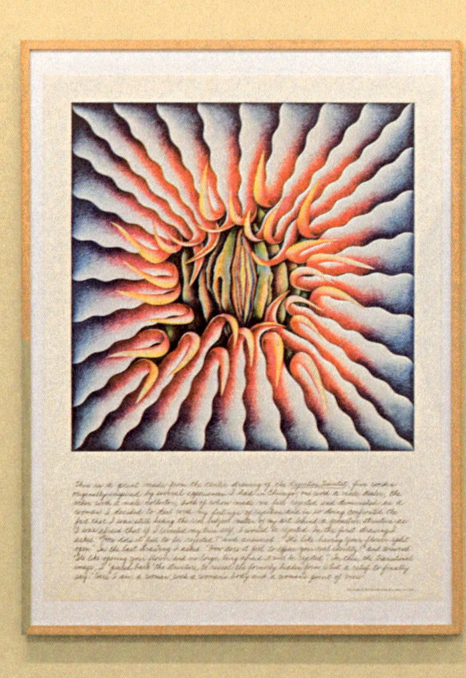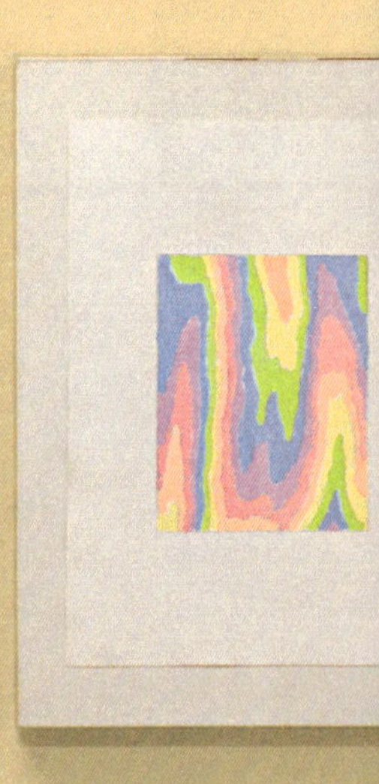

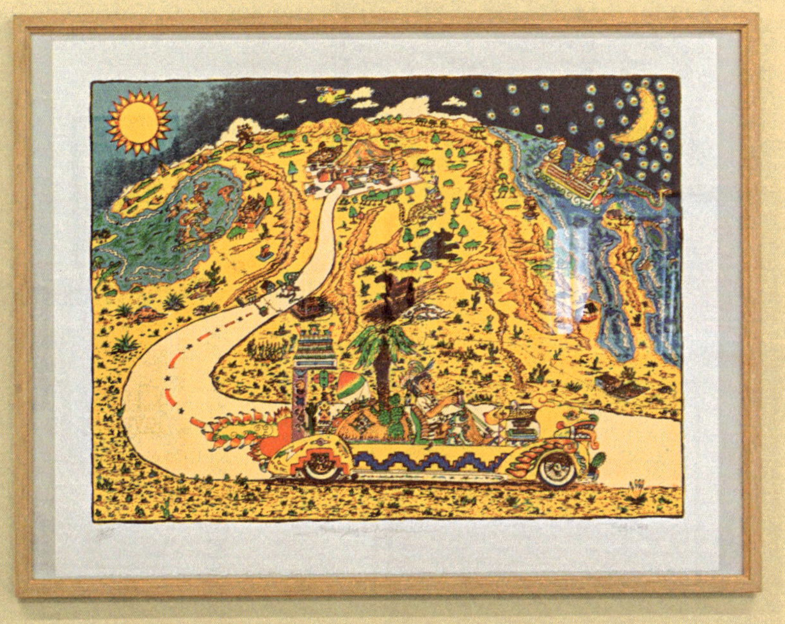 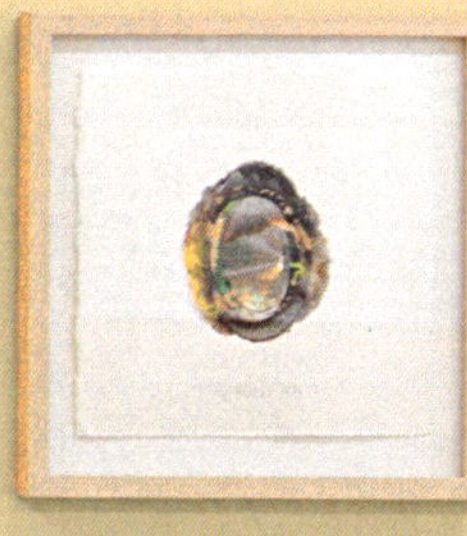

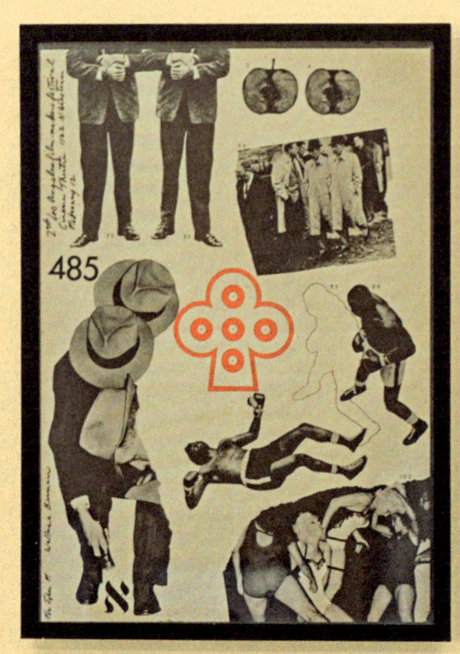

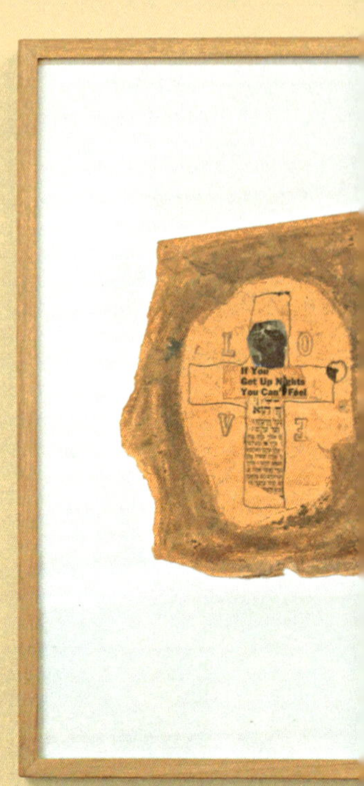
LOVE
If You
Get Up Nights
You Can Feel

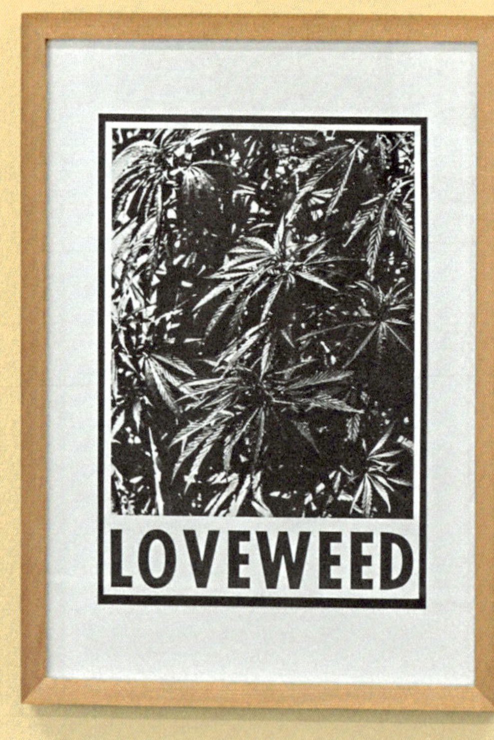
LOVEWEED

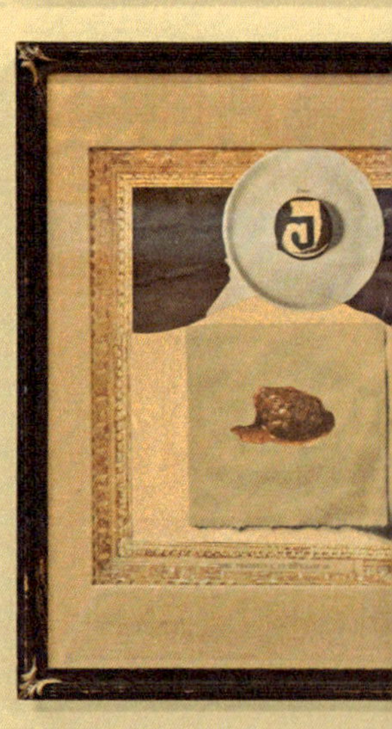

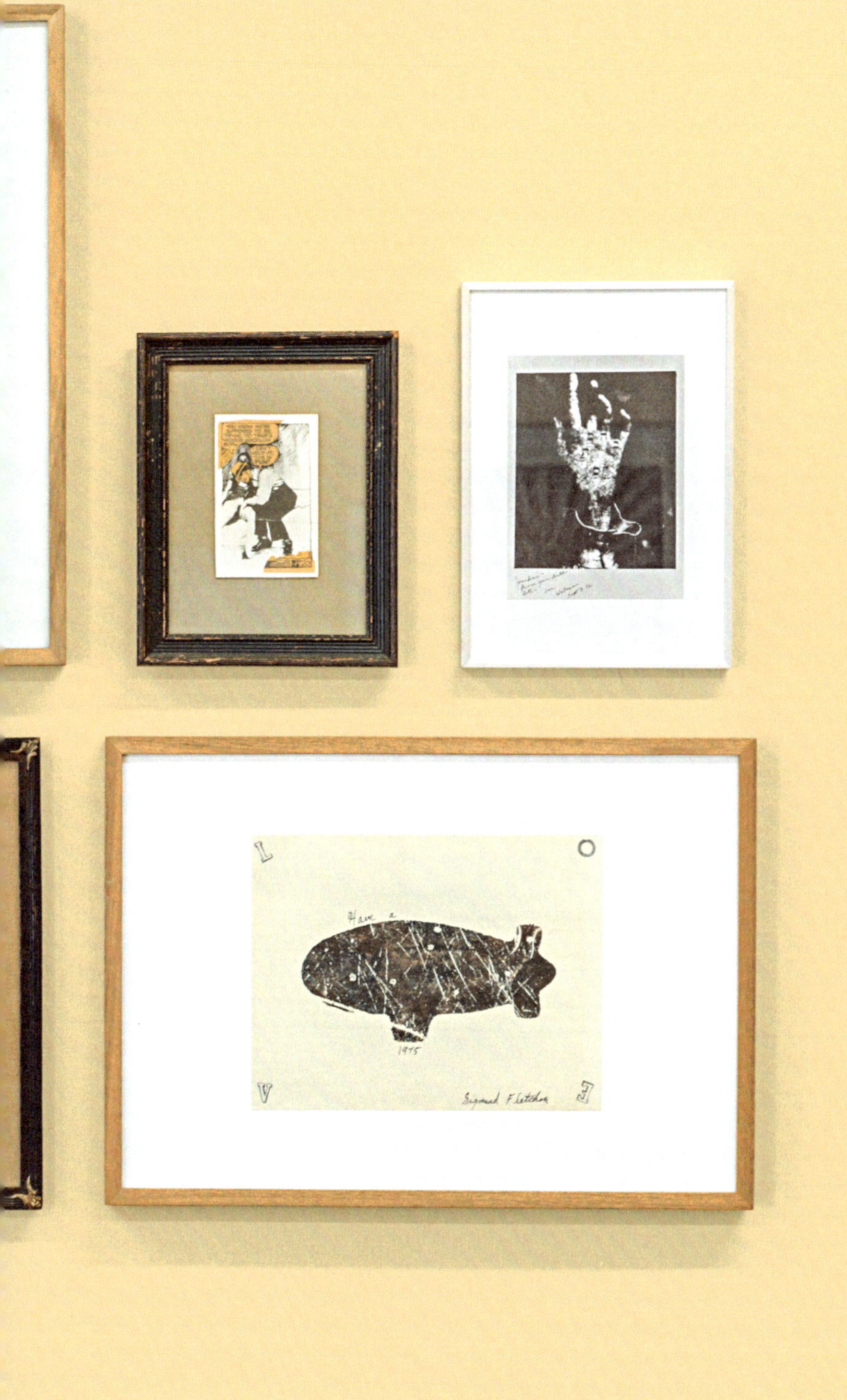

TABLE OF CONTENTS

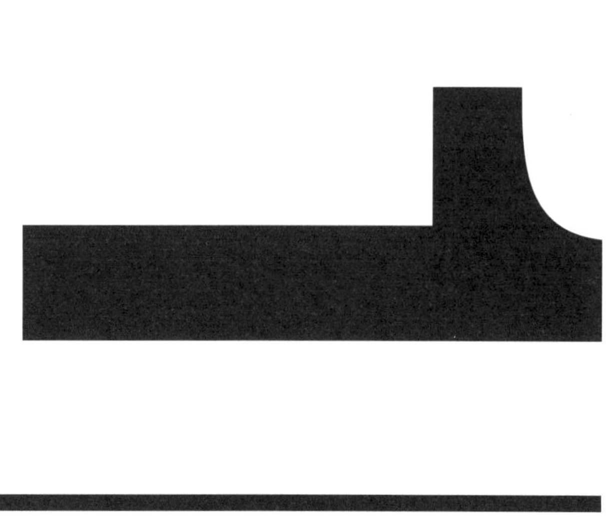
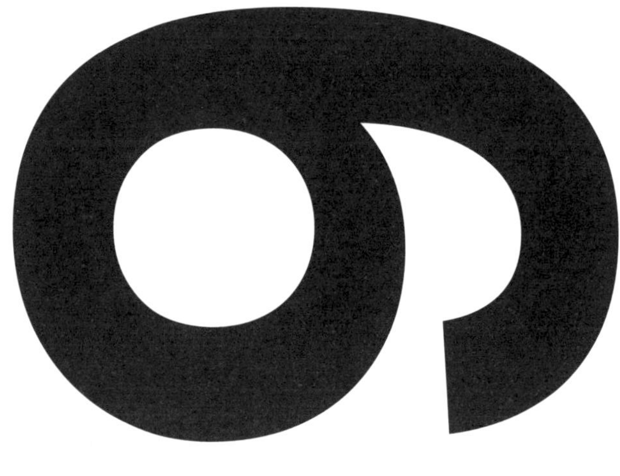

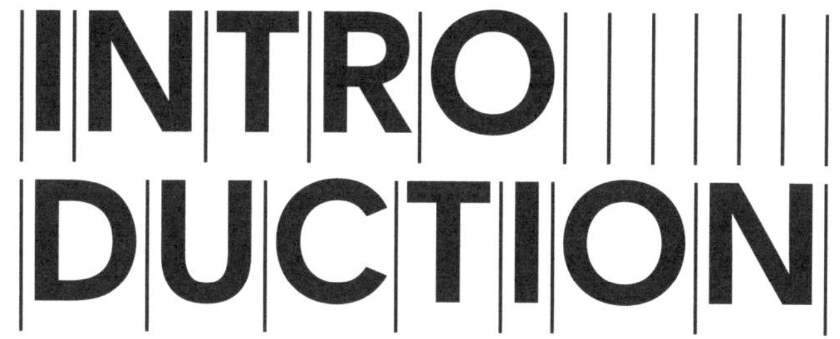

INTRO DUCTION

Lionel Bovier

Hal Glicksman (b. 1937) was an important figure on the Los Angeles art scene in the 1960s and 1970s, curating bold exhibitions at the Pomona College Art Gallery; the Art Gallery at the University of California, Irvine (UCI); and the Otis Art Institute Gallery.

As a young student living in Venice Beach, Glicksman witnessed the Beat Generation firsthand and came into contact with artists such as Ben Talbert and Fred Mason. He also developed an interest in the work of George Herms, Wallace Berman, and Bruce Conner from the San Francisco scene. In 1968, Glicksman co-curated an exhibition of California Assemblage art with Hopps and John Coplans, helping the movement gain recognition among traditional art circles.

Starting in 1969, Glicksman became heavily involved in site-specific art projects at Pomona College. Although Michael Asher and Tom Eatherton are conventionally associated with two markedly different trends—Institutional Critique and Light and Space—they share a propensity for transforming the exhibition space in a way that provides visitors with a singular experience. Writing about California installation art, Italian critic Germano Celant noted: "These spaces (...) being permeated with emptiness and nothingness, immobility and non-images, do in fact bring on a state of concentration and inward meditation. They seem to take one into non-matter, but this sensation turns out to be 'full of things.'"

In 1972, as director of the art gallery at UCI, Glicksman curated shows of Assemblage and Chicano art while continuing to explore site-specific art through exhibitions of the works of Bruce Nauman, Larry Bell, Peter Alexander, and Jane Reynolds.

There are strong parallels between Glicksman's career and the MAMCO collection. For one thing, both are associated with Conceptual artists such as Maria Nordman, Sol LeWitt, and Rosemarie Castoro. They also share strong ties with Guy de Cointet, an artist whom Glicksman and his wife Mary Ann Duganne worked with throughout their careers, and many of whose works are held in the museum's collection. In 2022, the Glicksmans made their first donation to MAMCO. In 2023, they donated another, larger set of works to be shared between the museum and the Kunsthaus Biel Centre d'art in Bienne (KBCB). In addition to presenting a visual overview of the California art scene, this generous donation provides insight into the prevailing culture and its famous—and lesser-known—figures through a range of documents.

20

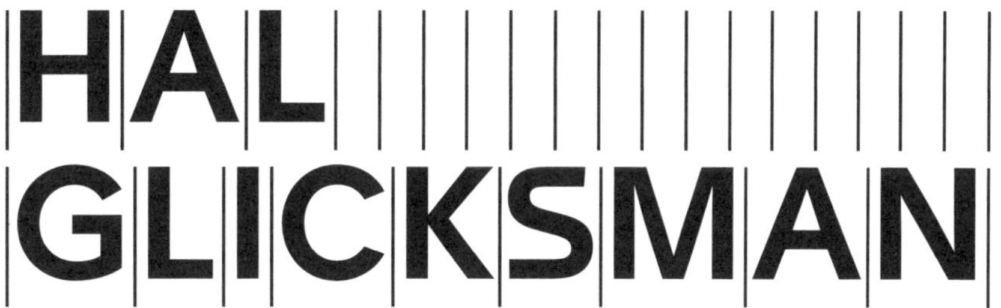

Interview with Hal Glicksman
by Paul Bernard and Julien Fronsacq (April 2023)

Where did you study?

HG   At UCLA. I grew up in Beverly Hills, very close to it. I was lucky to get in as I had no idea what I wanted to do. My family wanted me to be either a lawyer or a doctor. I enrolled in political science for one semester, but I hated it. Then I took some classes in philosophy.

What was your first encounter with art?

HG   I was looking around for things to do and I saw there was a class in modern art. I was only a Sophomore around that time and it was supposed to be a class for third-year students. So I went to the professor, Fred White, who generously agreed to let me take it. I fell in love with modern art. He was a great teacher and a good painter, too. I noticed that he had a lot of students helping install exhibitions. I asked him if I could volunteer as well, and he said: "No, you have to be paid." He offered me my first experiences with art and that's when I decided I wanted to make my profession out of it. Then, I made friends with artists like Ben Talbert.

Around the same time, were you also connected with writers?

HG   Yes, mostly poets. They were also making collages and giving them away to each other. I offered a little group of them to the Smithsonian Institution later on. By 1957, I'd heard of the Ferus Gallery, where Edward Kienholz and Walter and Shirley Hopps showed Abstract Expressionism, the Beat Generation, and the Assemblagists scene. I befriended Walter and started collaborating with him. He wasn't a curator at the Pasadena Museum at the time, but he was asked to organize some exhibitions there. He hired me and my friend Ben Talbert to work on an installation. When I graduated from UCLA, Fred White recommended me for a job at the Stanford Museum as a preparator. I did that for a year and then,

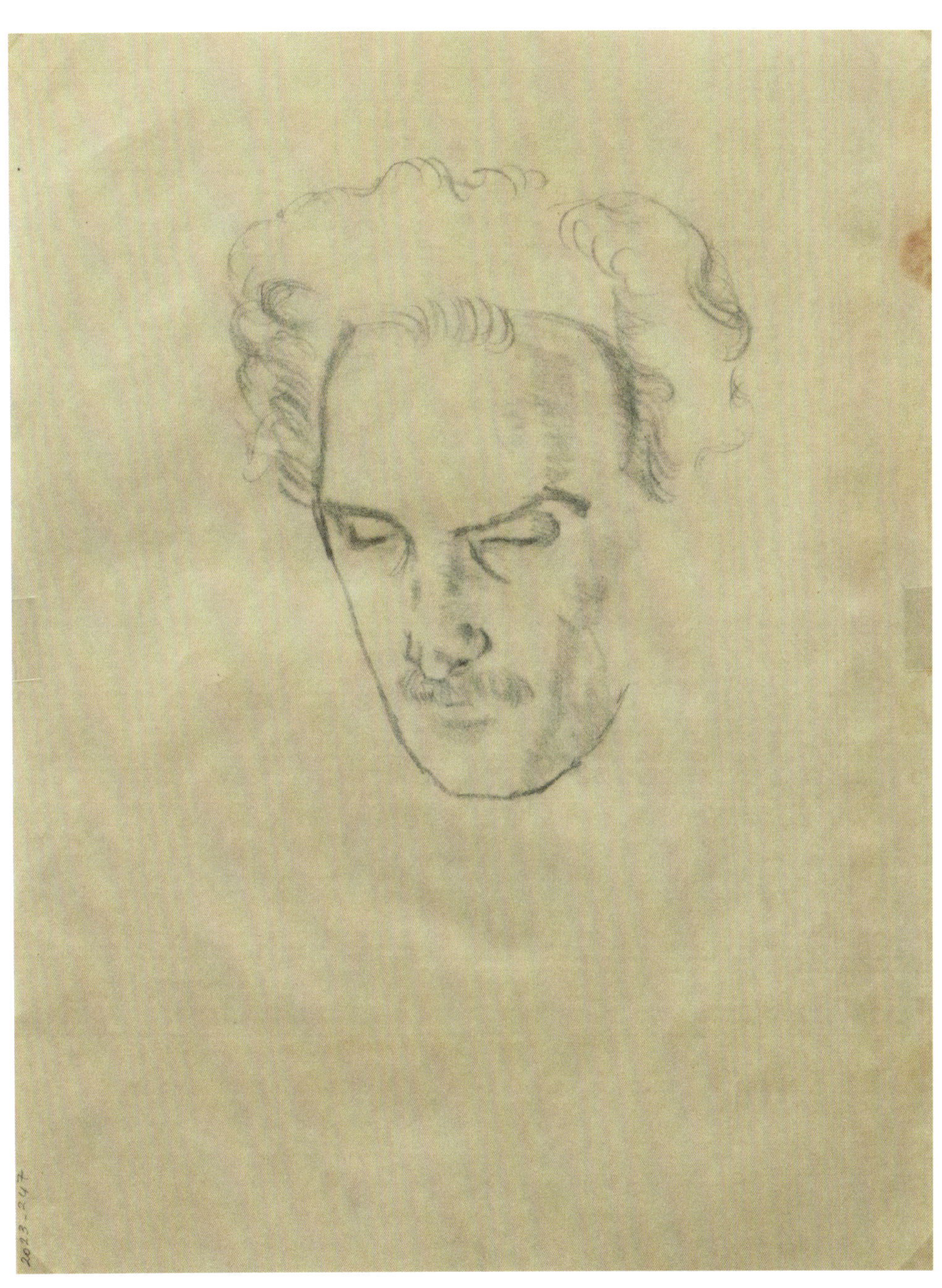

Jim Eller, *Portrait of Glicksman*, n.d.
coll. MAMCO, don Mary Ann et Hal Glicksman

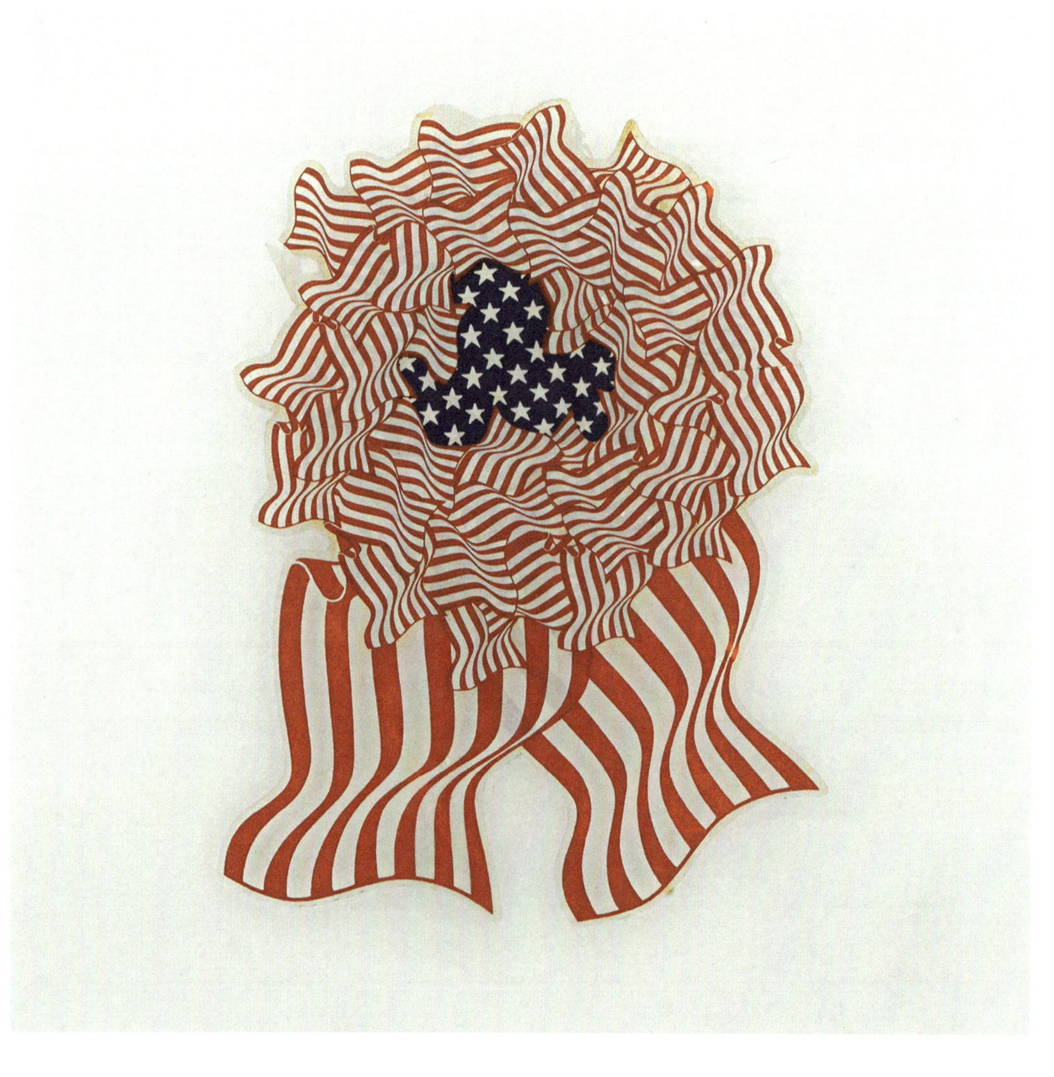

Hal Glicksman, *E Puribus Unum*, 1966
coll. MAMCO, don Mary Ann et Hal Glicksman

one night, Walter Hopps said: "Good news! The board approved a full-time preparator position and I would like you to do it. Can you start working on the Duchamp exhibition immediately?"

The Duchamp exhibition [Pasadena Museum of Art, 1963] was an important retrospective and the last show during his life, right?

HG   Yes. I think it was his biggest retrospective to date. It was a very interesting and well-done exhibition. We worked day and night without sleeping, just taking little naps on benches. It was insane. But we made Duchamp very happy! When we met him, we were sitting in the garden in our sweaty t-shirts, and he came to shake our hands—he was so gracious! The museum was a sleepy place before Walter got there, and it hadn't been maintained for years. It had mostly small rooms and only two big galleries: we painted one of them white and built free-standing walls to add six little spaces in the second one.

Do you remember how Duchamp was received in California and why he agreed to be exhibited in a "sleepy" museum, as you put it? Was his relationship with Walter Hopps that strong?

HG   In the 1930s and 1940s, around the influential presence of Walter Conrad Arensberg and his wife, there was a group of collectors in Los Angeles who had works by Surrealists and Cubists, as well as by German Expressionists. A collection of German Expressionist paintings and works by Paul Klee ended up in the Pasadena Museum, and that gave them connections with international museums and credentials within the art world. I worked there from 1963 to 1969 and they held extraordinary exhibitions within this period of time. Walter left in 1967 or 1968, after his Joseph Cornell show, and he was replaced by James Demetrion. During my time there, there were only five people running the museum. It wasn't that huge but, I mean, it was a lot for us. When I was asked to become the director of

Pomona College Gallery, I said: "You know, I'm just the preparator at Pasadena." But Mowry Baden replied: "No, I hear from the artists that you are the one who does everything." And, to a certain extent, it was true: Walter would spend an hour on the phone making the deal with an artist or a museum, and we would do everything else—bring the show in, ship it in, hang it in, and prepare the catalog.

When you started at Pomona, had you already curated any shows?

HG   Only one. John Coplans, who was the director at UC Irvine, asked me if I could do a show of my friends, who were mostly Assemblage artists. So I did *Assemblage in California* (University Art Gallery, UC Irvine, 1968). It included Bruce Conner, Edward Kienholz, Wallace Berman, and George Herms, who are all well-known names now, but also Fred Mason and Ben Talbert. In the catalog, there were essays by both Hopps and Coplans. Before becoming the director at Pomona, I had also done the installation of a series of Light and Space artists who John Coplans had invited: Larry Bell, Doug Wheeler, and Robert Irwin. But that was as a pre-parator. I also worked for, I think, six or eight months on the *Art and Technology* show at LACMA [Los Angeles County Museum of Art, 1971]. But when Mowry Baden invited me to run the gallery at Pomona College, that was my first time being in charge. It included teaching a course and making a program for the gallery.

It had no collection?

HG   A very small collection: just things that had been given by faculty and students.

How did you start the exhibition program?

HG   The gallery had three rooms: an entrance, in which you could just hang some paintings, plus a large gallery and a small room.

I made the large gallery into a space for Light and Space artists and installations. The small room was available to students to study and meditate: there was always someone sitting in there, looking at a Robert Irwin I had installed. It was very spiritual. At the time, I was living in Pasadena and studios were cheap, so I met with the little community of artists who were living there. Lloyd Hamrol, who shared a space with Judy Chicago, had made a beautiful piece in his studio: a big cube made out of red plastic and lit by a tiny filament, almost invisible. I said: "Jeez, could you do that in Pomona?" And he replied: "Well, I don't like to do the same things again, this was made for this particular space." I offered him a six-week installation slot and he agreed. He came to work in what he called "the artists' gallery," because it was like a residency for each artist who exhibited there, and he did several works. I didn't even see some of them: he'd put it up for one day, show it to a few students, then take it down. He finally ended up with a piece that lasted just a week, with balloons and water [ILL. P. 28–29]. Because the balloons didn't hold their air for very long, it just sort of faded away. Then Michael Asher did something great: he put a wall at a diagonal in the office space, through the hallway and into the big space—it completely changed how those spaces interacted [*Installation,* 1970, ILL. P. 117].

How did you meet Michael Asher?

HG   He was still a student at Irvine, Walter liked him, and Claire Copley made him his assistant. So I knew him as an art student. He was the son of an important art collector and he'd grown up with art. He knew most of the artists of the time. Betty Asher was a curator at LACMA for a while. She also had a gallery for a while and was one of the founders of the Fellows of Contemporary Art, a big art collector group in LA. So Michael was an insider. I just did it on trust that he would do something interesting. And it turned out to be this wonderful piece.

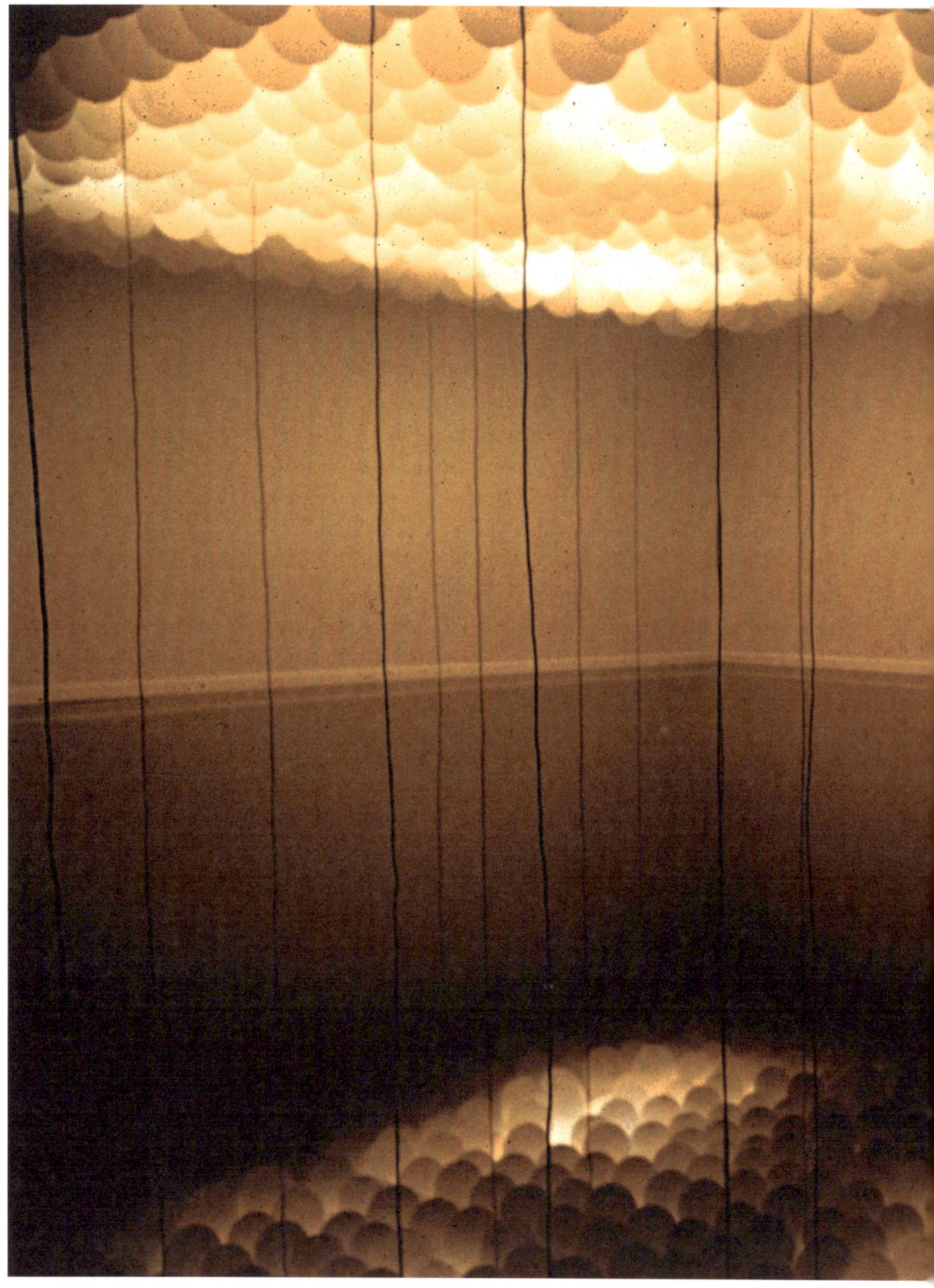

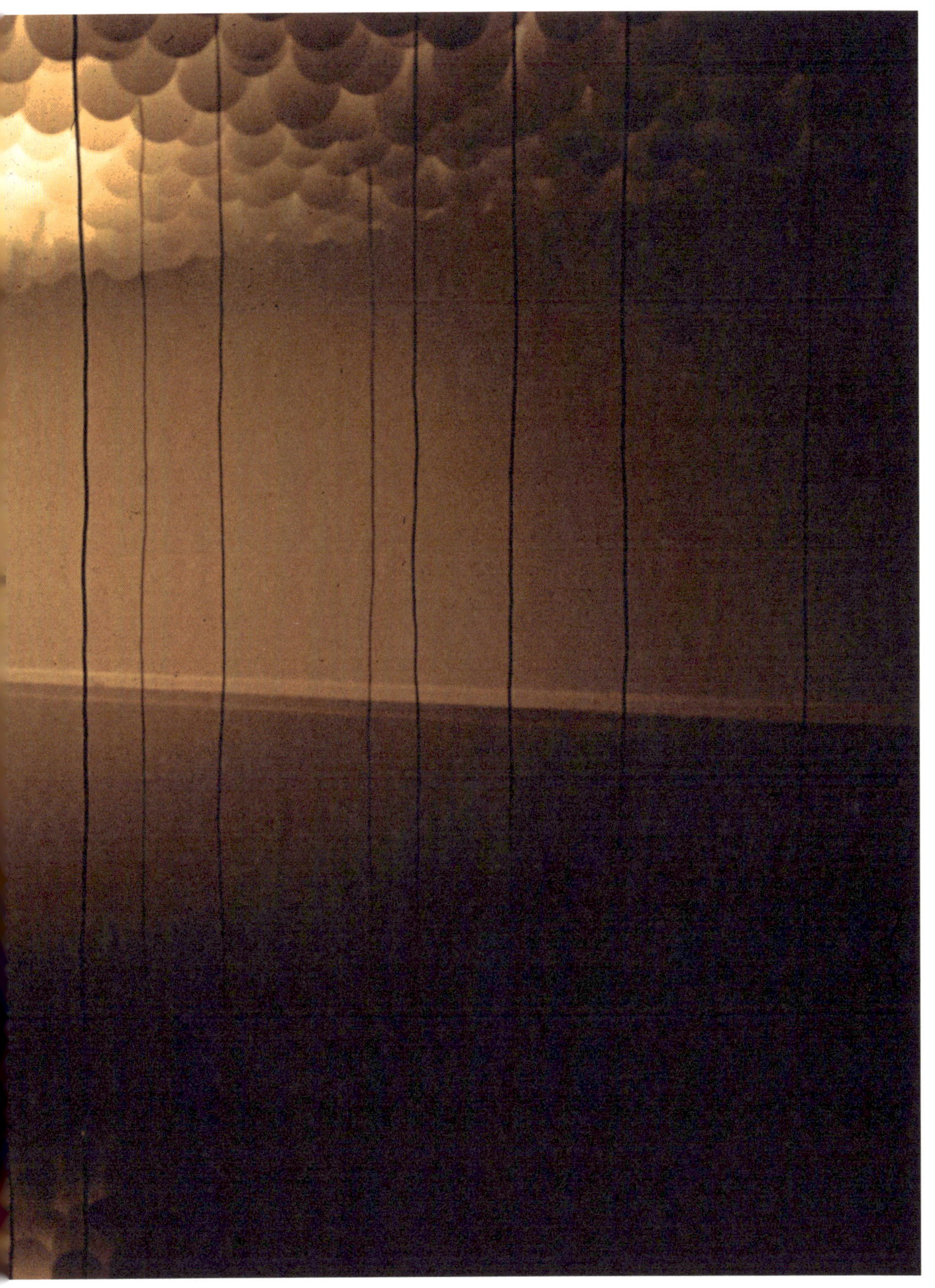

Llyod Hamrol, Pomona College Museum of Art, 1969
Gift of Hal Glicksman. Getty Research Institute, Los Angeles (2009.M.5)

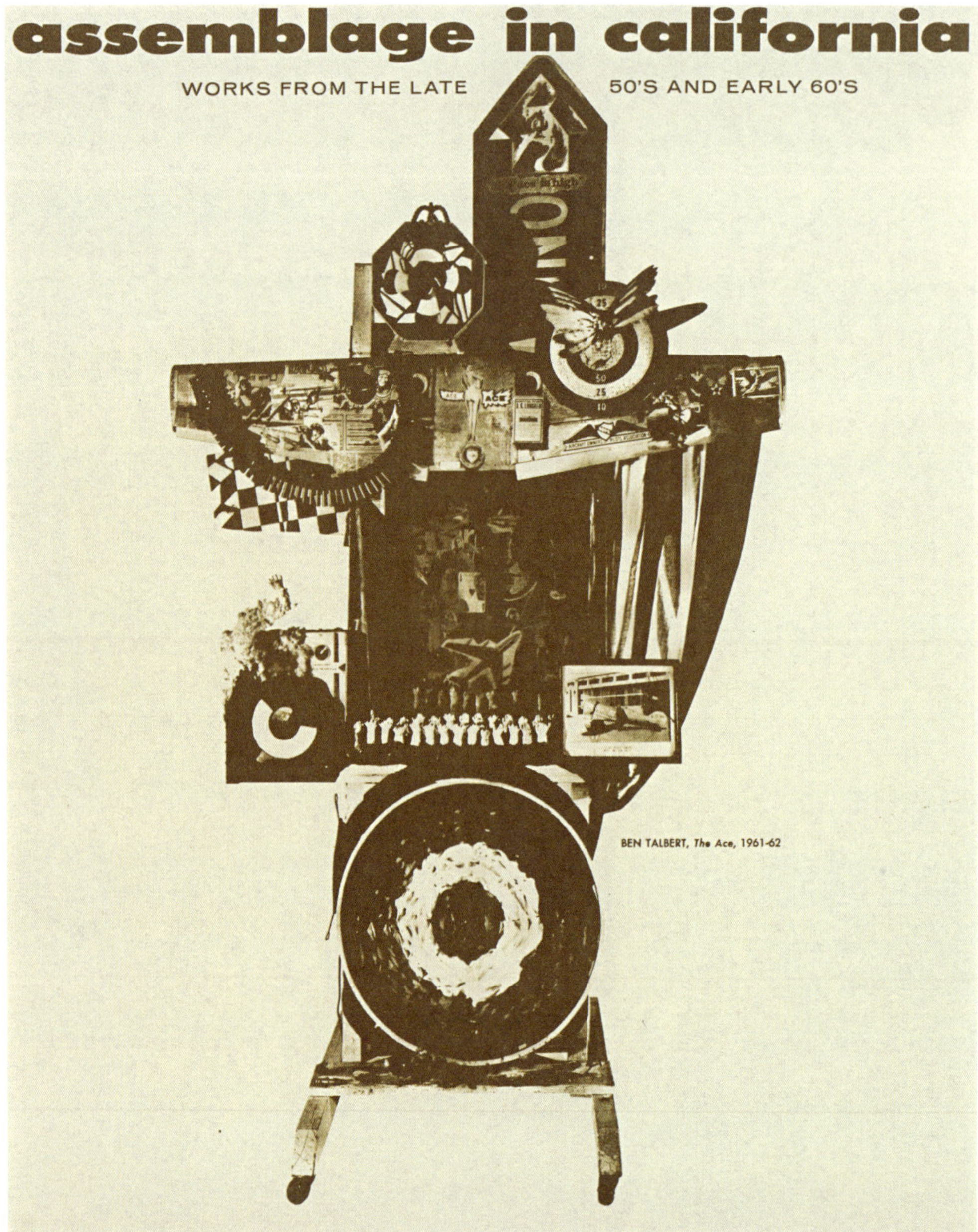

Ben Talbert, exhibition poster *Assemblage in California,* University of California, Irvine, 1968
coll. MAMCO, don Mary Ann et Hal Glicksman

Who else did you invite to show there?

HG   Tom Eatherton, who was a close friend. Tom had wonderful ideas but not much practical knowledge. So I did about half of the work, inventing this piece called *Rise* then installing it. It was a very beautiful work: it was built inside the big room—two curving walls of blue light diffracted by layers of white plastic and nylon [*Rise*, Pomona College Art Gallery, 1970, ILL. P. 80–81]. I did a show called *Movie Palace Modern: Drawings of A.B. Heinsbergen, Photographs from Mott Studios* [Pomona College Art Gallery, 1969], which was taken up by the Smithsonian as a traveling exhibition. They toured it for three years. I also organized a project on the Chicano graffiti scene. It didn't look like New York graffiti: it was much more calligraphic, you know; it was inventive alphabets and things like that. I had some students at Pomona College go out and photograph graffiti on different kinds of buildings. Some very good students also had student shows there, like Lewis Baltz, Chris Burden, and James Turrell.

How long did you work there?

HG   Between 1969 and 1970. So I did all of those things in one academic year! Then Walter called me. He had worked as a guest curator at the Menil Foundation and landed a job as the curator of the Washington Gallery of Modern Art in Washington, D.C. It was encountering financial difficulties and it merged with the Corcoran Gallery of Art. So Walter became the curator of the Corcoran Gallery. Eventually, he was asked to be the director, but somehow they understood he didn't really direct things. So Walter hired me as associate director. I thought: "Oh my God, I'll go to a major museum, I'll be an associate director, I'll live on the East Coast, and I'll wear suits every day," and all this kind of stuff. I went to the Corcoran and it was a disaster from day one! I mean, you can't imagine the wonderful things we did, great shows really, but the building was so old, it needed all kinds of repairs. The museum was always in serious debt, and the trustees were very old—and Republicans. Walter Hopps ended up being fired, and then a horrible person from the board took over as director, although that didn't last too long either!

Which exhibitions do you remember from your time at the Corcoran?

HG   Thomas Wilfred was one I especially enjoyed. He was the builder of the Clavilux, an organ that he did shows of, you know, in the 1920s and 1930s [*Thomas Wilfred: Lumia, A Retrospective Exhibition,* Corcoran Gallery of Art, 1971].

An "orgue chromatique"?

HG   Yes. It was playing sound and colors. He realized that he wouldn't be able to compose for this, so he made a stationary one that worked automatically. He also made a big machine for a shopping mall: it was supposed to shine at the building at night. But it wasn't bright enough and the street lights and everything sort of washed it out, so the owner gave it to the Corcoran for this show to become part of the collection. And you know, after, with the changes, and people coming and going, they lost it!

How big was it?

HG   It was the size of a refrigerator. It was supposed to project onto a wall, so we made a huge rear-projection screen for it. It filled an entire gallery, and that's the cover of the catalog. One of his most wonderful pieces, and it disappeared.

After your Corcoran experience, you moved back to Los Angeles?

HG   Yes. The dean of UC Irvine offered me a job as gallery director, but I still had a few months left in Washington, D.C. And I made

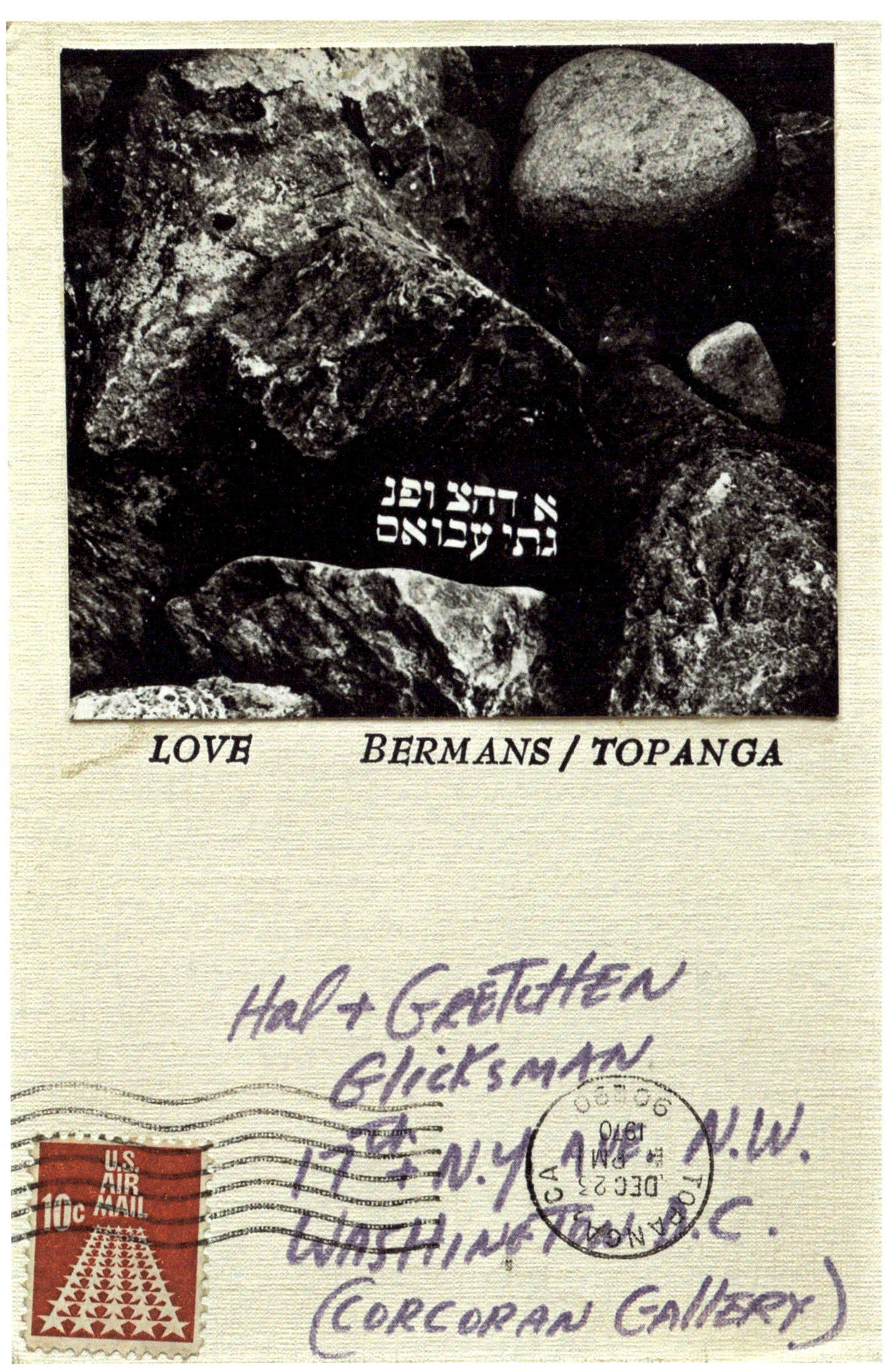

Wallace Berman, carte postcard, 1970
coll. MAMCO, don Mary Ann et Hal Glicksman

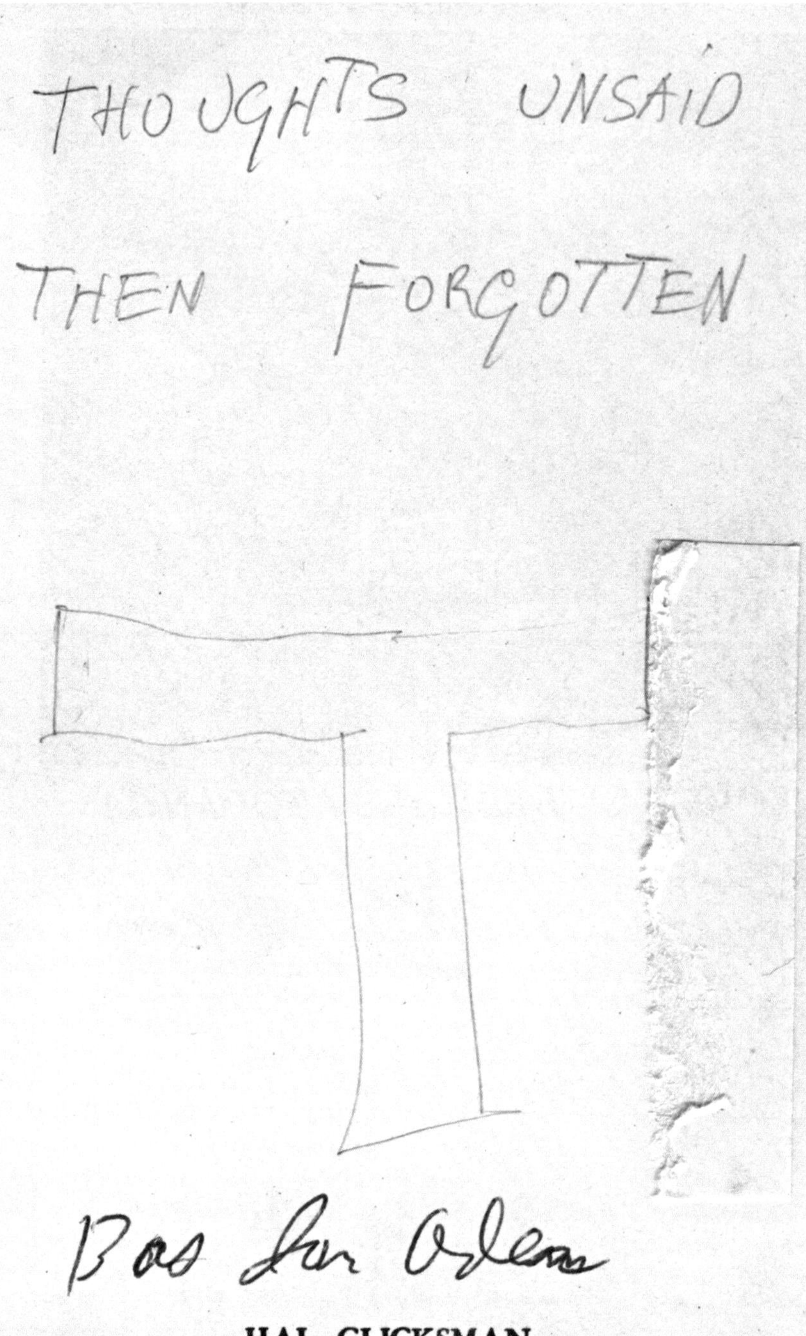

Business card of Hal Glicksman autographed by Bas Jan Ader, ca. 1972–1973
coll. MAMCO, don Mary Ann et Hal Glicksman

up my mind that I would find an exhibition under the nose of all these curators and museum directors in D.C.—one that they were not aware of. So I went to the Pentagon, which at that time you could just walk into, and they had on the wall illustrations of World War II that *Life* magazine had commissioned. During the war, they were not allowed to print any photographs, especially if they showed a dead American, so they commissioned 1930s painters like Reginald Marsh. I noticed that if you took one of these artists who painted the countryside and old barns and things like that, and you put them in front of a submarine, they'd end up producing a painting of a submarine that looked like the Photorealism that was going on in the 1960s. Their war illustrations somehow echoed the work of popular artists of that time who painted store fronts and shiny things. It was also a fun show because I got to spend time in the Library of Congress and, you know, as I was picking through, I saw they had a collection of World War II posters in mint condition. I really made a great show.

What did you gather for the show? Did you invite artists to produce paintings?

HG   No, it was just World War II illustrations. This was my first show at Irvine, with material I'd found in Washington D.C. It was a way to tap into the mainstream, even if I don't like the word, but with things people were not looking at and found naïve and folk.

Do you remember the title of that show?

HG   *World War II* [laughs]. It was the middle of the Cold War, so it was politically loaded to refer to World War II. And to show World War II illustrations to a bunch of liberal students in Irvine was definitely politically incorrect! I stayed at Irvine for three years. I mostly did installations, Light and Space works, and some other things. Tom Eatherton had a show there, and so did Larry Bell. He wanted to produce a sound installation: a wall of

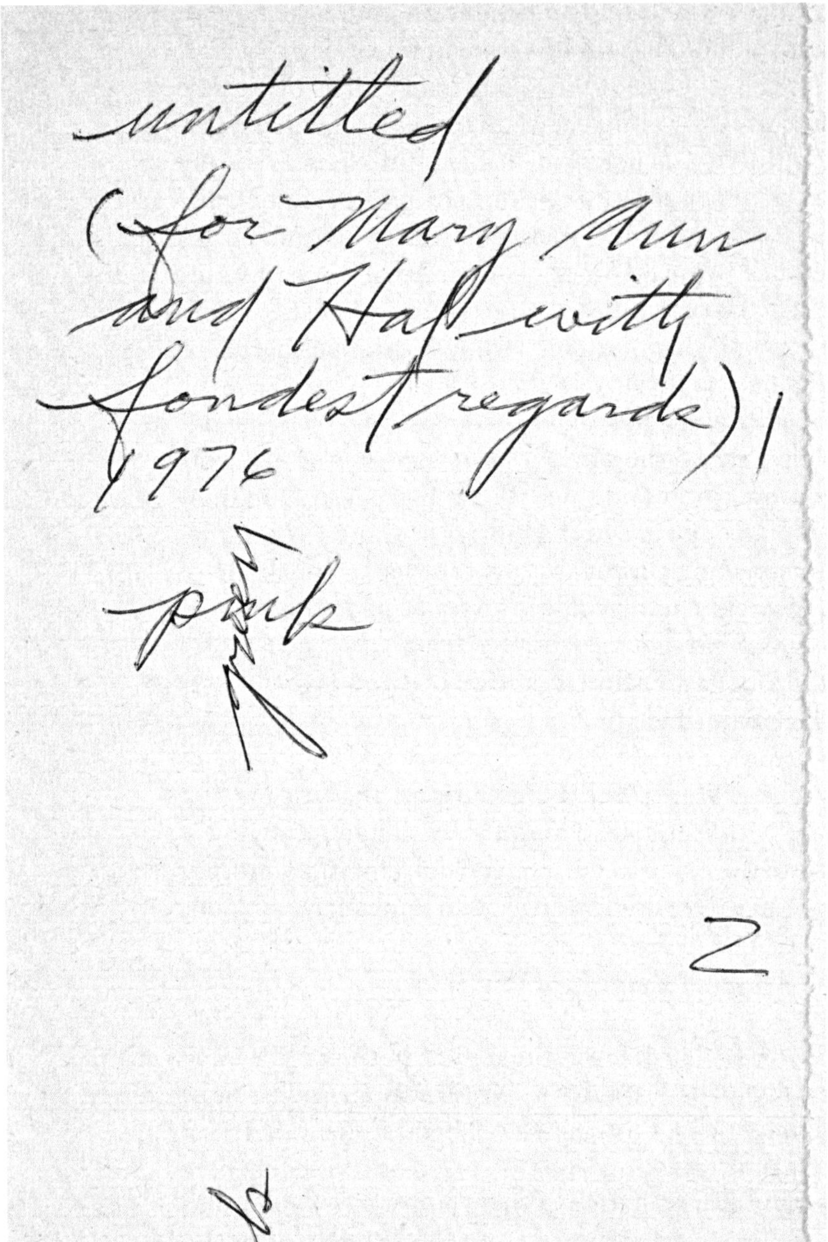

untitled
(for Mary Ann
and Harr ewith
fondest regards) 1
1976

pink

2

green

Dan Flavin, drawing on a paper towel, 1976
Fondation Collection Centre PasquArt

sound. He started building a room with sound-absorbing material, experimented with speakers, and so on. And on the last day of the installation, he packed everything up and said: "You know, I didn't come up with anything." He did a poster with the gallery plan and a picture of his shoe going into his ear. Artist Eric Orr and physics professor Richard Ballard made a computer map of the sound levels in the gallery as Larry Bell left it.

How did you meet Mary Ann Duganne, who became your wife?

HG   I met Mary Ann in 1975. She was friends with Larry Bell and Guy de Cointet. Guy asked her to be in his plays [*At Sunrise a Cry was Heard,* performed by Mary Ann Duganne, Biltmore Hotel, Los Angeles, in conjunction with the American Theater Convention, 1976]. I had shown Guy at Irvine and Mary Ann knew that I was friends with Larry. We met, we became friends, and we got married. When I met her son, John, who had cerebral palsy, I saw that he was always eager to do something. You know, he was a very happy kid even though he couldn't walk, he couldn't feed himself, and all these things. But he was still anxious to do something. So I bought him a little TV, with a TV changer, and I made a wooden box, so that all he had to do was touch it with his hand and he could change the channels! Later, I got the idea, probably from the *Art and Technology* project, that he could use a personal computer, which was a brand-new thing at the time. And they were not for kids—especially not for children with disabilities. So I asked a college kid to write a program that would allow John to use it. He liked to play with it, especially with the early games. We played them together and I thought that I had to learn how to program. And that's what I did!

Is that why you stopped working in the art world?

HG   In 1978, Otis College of Art and Design, where I was teaching, became affiliated with New York's Parsons School of Design.

They didn't want Light and Space anymore. They wanted fashion and illustration, you know. They didn't want me anymore. So I left. Mary Ann started teaching and, when I was 43, I think, I met someone who was starting a computer company. He knew that I had worked in museums and had done books and he said: "I'm gonna sell computer games and computer books and I need an editor for the computer books. Would you take it on?" I said: "Well, you know, I don't know much about computers." He replied: "You know about how to read and write, and they don't." I ended up in this little company. It only lasted for a couple of years, but this is how I got completely out of the art business.

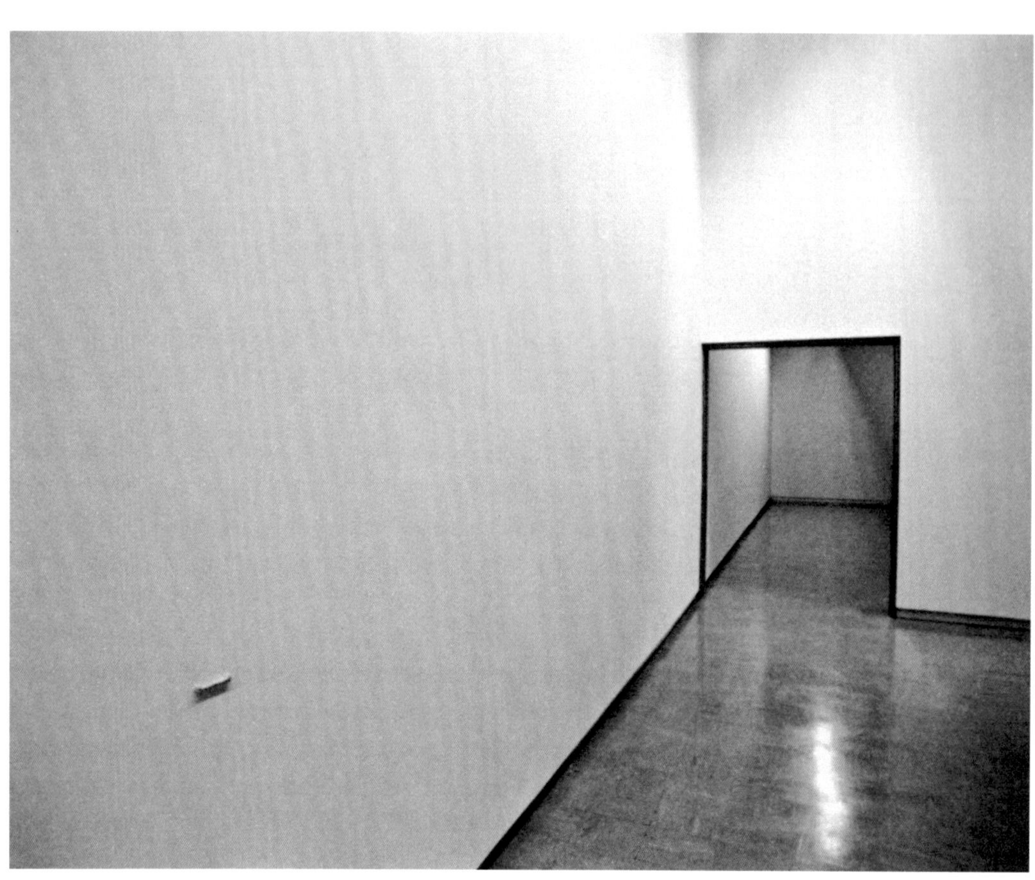

Installation by Richard Tuttle, Otis Art Institute, 1976
Gift of Hal Glicksman. Getty Research Institute, Los Angeles (2009.M.5)

Guy de Cointet, *I can't live here any longer*, circa 1980
Fondation Collection Centre PasquArt

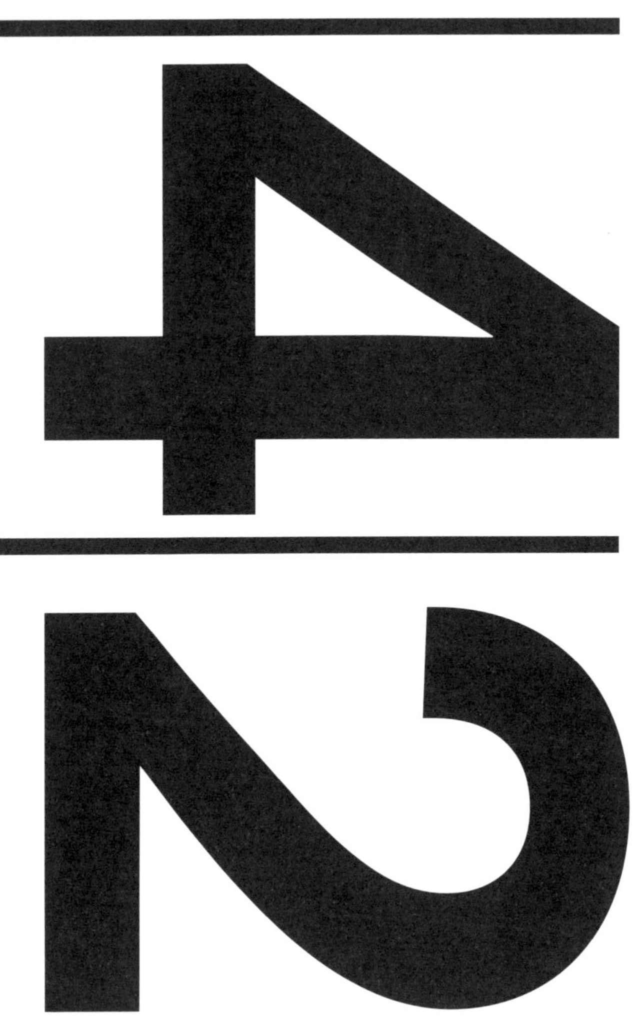

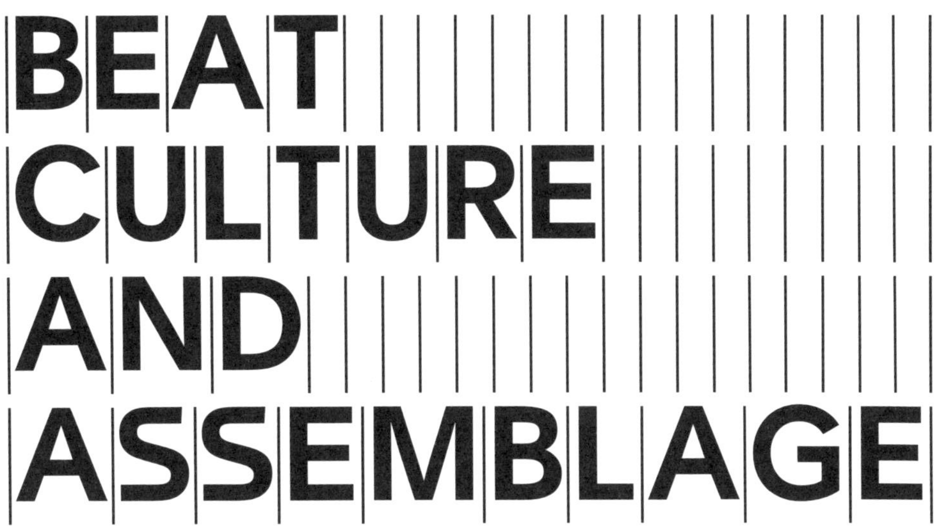

Anne Giffon-Selle

Literature, and poetry in particular, has consistently been one of the most powerful connectors between painters and Assemblage artists: both groups have retained a strong attachment to the form of poetry that, starting in the 1940s, would go on to shape the cultural landscape of California, and of San Francisco in particular. Over time, the Assemblage artists developed even closer ties than their predecessors did with the San Francisco Renaissance poets. Paradoxically, these poets' early artistic affinities were more with painting than with assemblage. They often characterized their experimental works using terms borrowed from abstract painting—such as "free form," "open form," and "field of action"[1]—while keeping company with both contemporary Assemblage artists and first- and second-wave Abstract Expressionists.

Bruce Conner's 1959 painting *Dark Brown*[2] was conceived as an abstract, matterist tribute to Michael McClure's poem of the same name. Rather than identifying with any artistic trend, Conner thought it more appropriate to use physical materials to honor a poem that was itself written in praise of painting. Poetry had a uniquely formative influence on Californian Assemblage. In *The Art of Assemblage,* William Seitz recalled that the earliest attempts at collage and free association in literature could be found in the letters of Arthur Rimbaud and Charles Baudelaire, in Stéphane Mallarmé's assembled fragments and typographical experiments, and in Guillaume Apollinaire's calligrams,[3] all of which were familiar references for exponents of the Assemblage movement. The Dada poets should also be added into the mix: Robert Motherwell's 1951 anthology placed a much greater emphasis on Dadaist writings than paintings, which occupied only a small portion of the book and, of course, were reproduced in black and white. Surrealist and Dadaist poetry therefore contained a literary seed that played a key role in the genesis of West Coast Assemblage—a marked contrast to the neo-Dadaist roots of its East Coast equivalent. As this nascent movement gained strength in the late 1940s, something of a literary revival occurred: because California still lacked an established art market—with its attendant galleries and museums—poetry came to dominate the cultural landscape, serving as an early template for plastic artists.

—Anne Giffon-Selle[4]

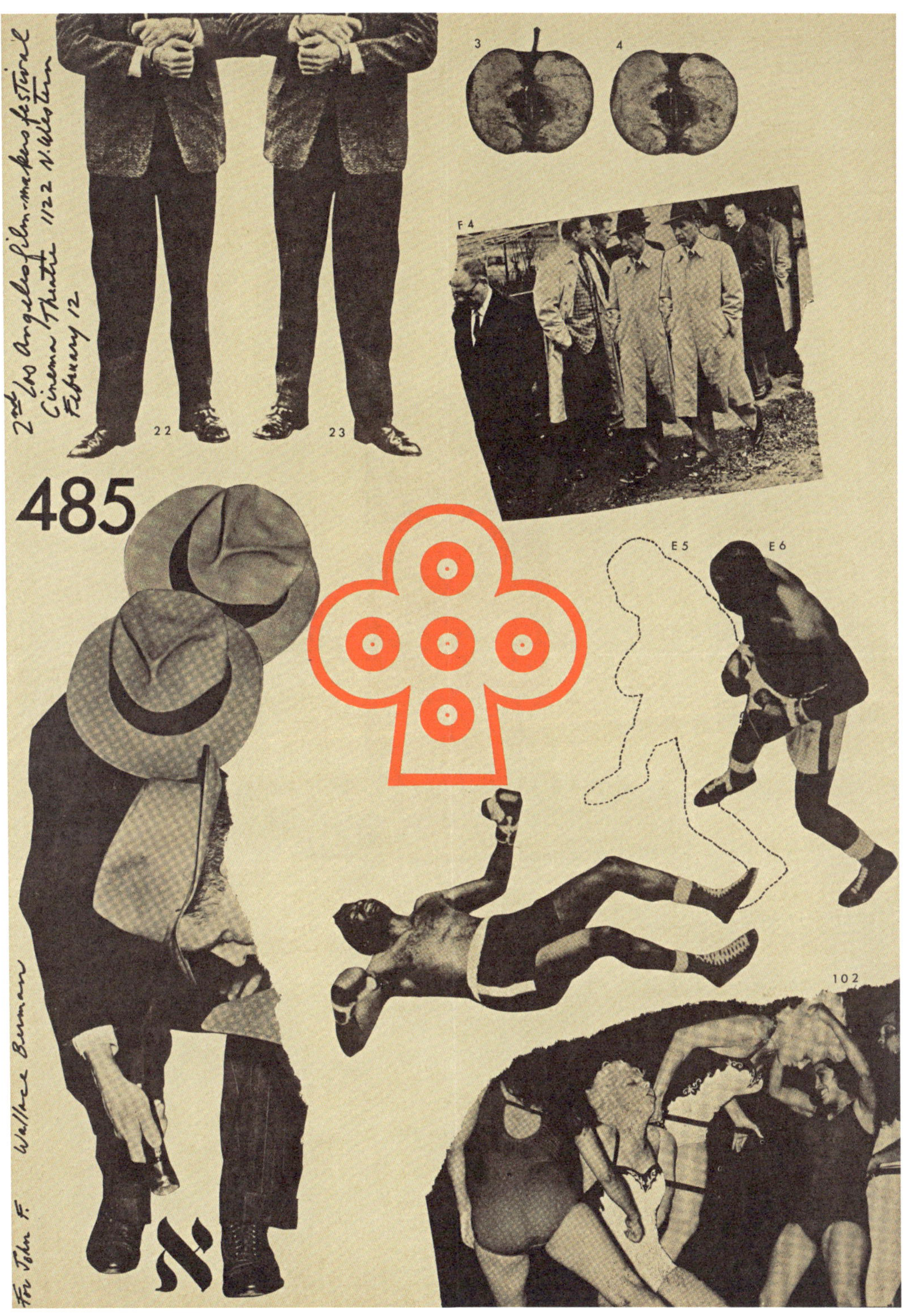

Wallace Berman, *2nd Los Angeles Filmmakers Festival*, 1963
Fondation Collection Centre PasquArt

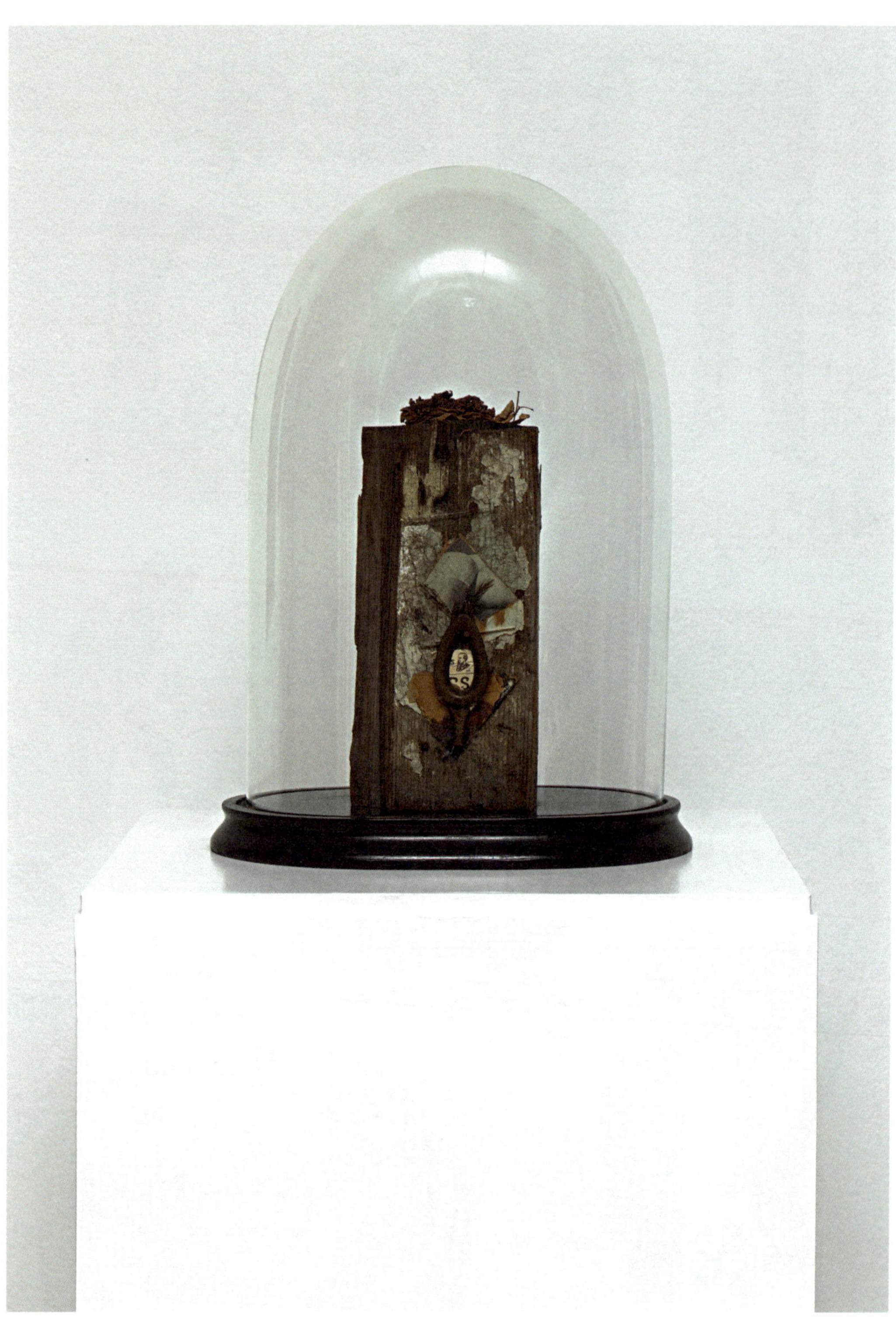

Fred Mason, *Untitled*, circa 1960
coll. MAMCO, don Mary Ann et Hal Glicksman

1   The idea of the "poem as a field of action" was first posited by William Carlos Williams during a lecture in 1948. The concept of "composition by field" was later developed by Charles Olson, while Robert Duncan expanded on the notion of "action." See Robert J. Bertholf, "The Concert: Robert Duncan Writing Out of Painting," in *Jess, a Grand Collage,* Albright–Knox Art Gallery, Buffalo, 1993, p. 74. Critic Alain Jouffroy drew a similar parallel between the "spilling out of the frame" characteristic of Abstract Expressionist painting (in this particular instance, the work of Jackson Pollock), and the linguistic excesses of the Beat poets. See Alain Jouffroy, preface to *La Poésie de la Beat Generation,* translated and introduced by Jean-Jacques Lebel, Paris, Denoël, 1965, p. 18.

2   Bruce Conner, *Dark Brown,* 1959; oil, shellac, fabric, costume jewelry, and aluminum paint on canvas with fur, San Francisco Museum of Modern Art.

3   William Seitz, "The Liberation of Words," *The Art of Assemblage,* MoMA, New York, 1961, p. 13–15.

4   Excerpt from "Le poème est un collage de réel. L'assemblage et la renaissance poétique," *Les astronautes du dedans,* MAMCO and Les presses du réel, Geneva, 2017, p. 49–50.

Anne Giffon-Selle

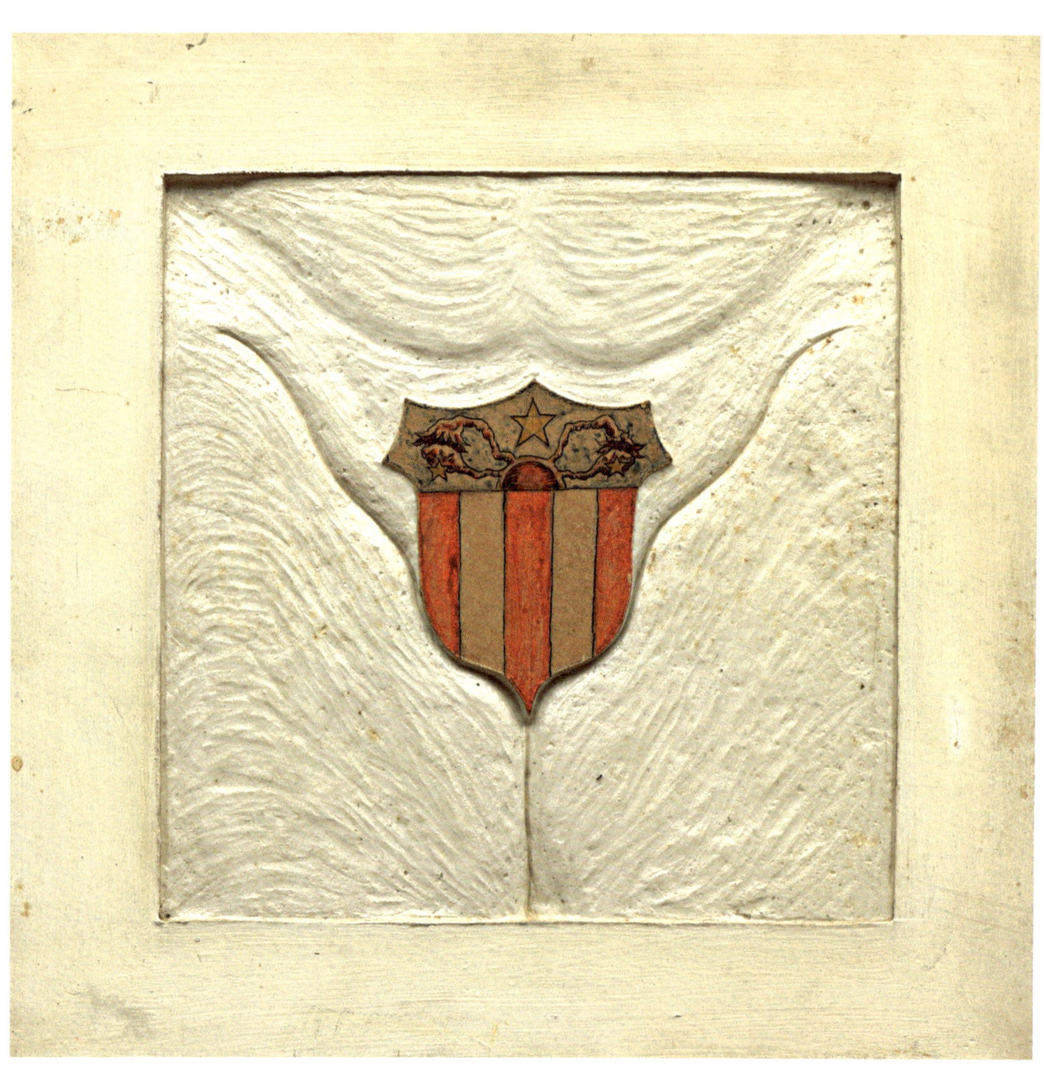

Ben Talbert, *Romulus & Remus*, n.d.
coll. MAMCO, don Mary Ann et Hal Glicksman

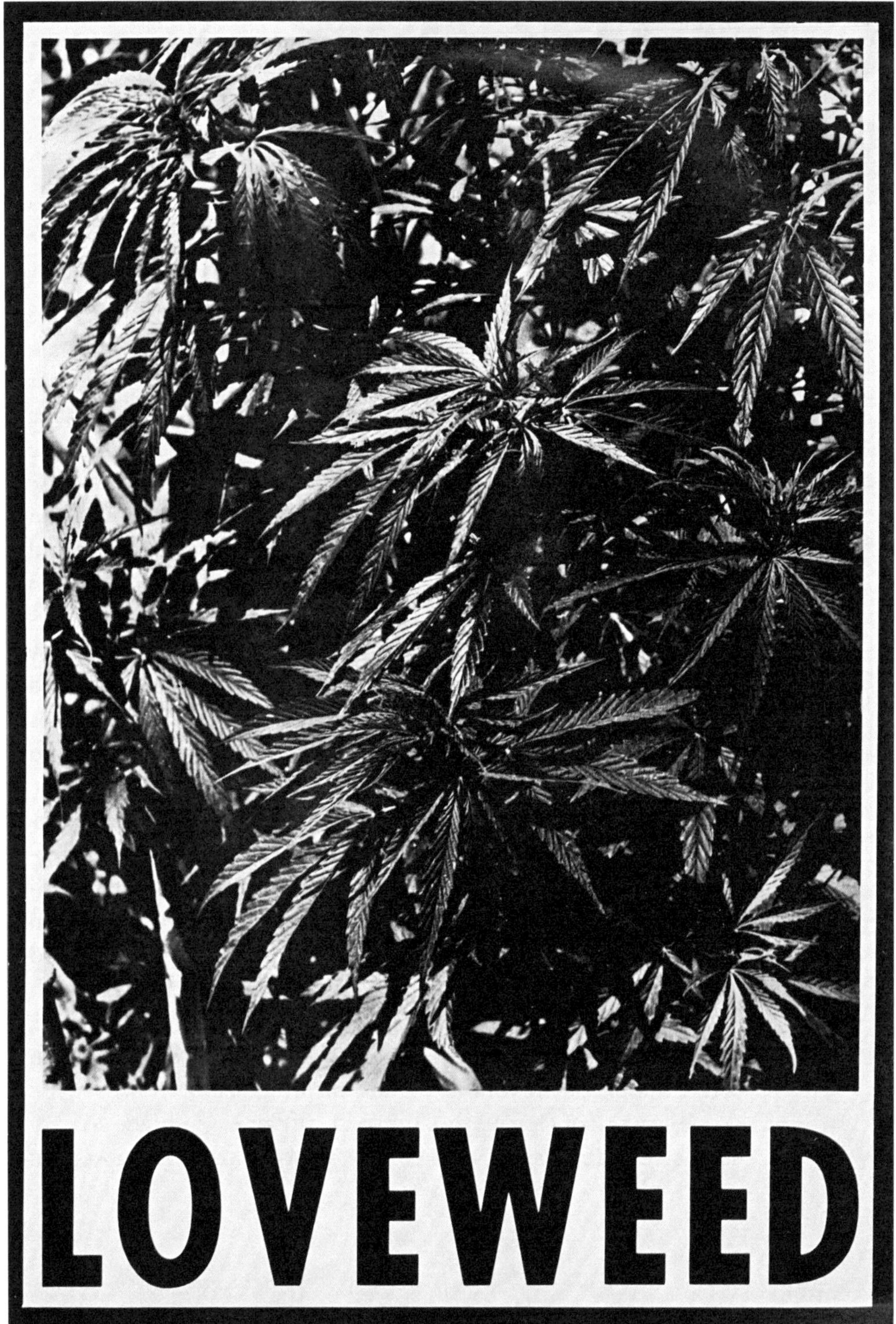

Wallace Berman, *Love Weed*, 1959
coll. MAMCO, don Mary Ann et Hal Glicksman

GEORGE HERMS

In 1956, George Herms (born in 1935 in Woodland, California; lives and works in Los Angeles) joined the ranks of the early Californian Assemblage artists. The youngest and only surviving member of the group, he retains memories of that time to this day. Jazz and poetry are essential to his creative process, just as they were for most of these artists—including Wallace Berman, his close associate and fellow lover of heteronyms. Herms even went on to publish the writings of his poet friends Michael McClure and Diane di Prima through The LOVE Press, his own imprint which he founded in 1957.

For Herms, creating assemblages out of discarded everyday objects is a critical reaction to the consumerist concept of "planned obsolescence" that first came to prominence in the United States in the late 1940s. But, above all, it is a "natural," mainstream and universally accessible activity.[1] He likens the cyclical, organic aspect of his artistic practice to gardening: a process character-ized by fragile raw materials and inevitable death, but also by per-petual rebirth. This affinity for the natural world shines through in Herms' work more than in the output of other Californian Assemblage artists, as evidenced by his frequent use of wood and in the weathered look bestowed upon his materials through their exposure to the elements. Through his focus on damaged, corroded and rusted objects, Herms writes the latest chapter in a tale that leads inexorably toward disintegration.

The work of Herms, the "hippiest" of the Assemblage artists,[2] is so steeped in a sense of love that, starting in the late 1950s, he

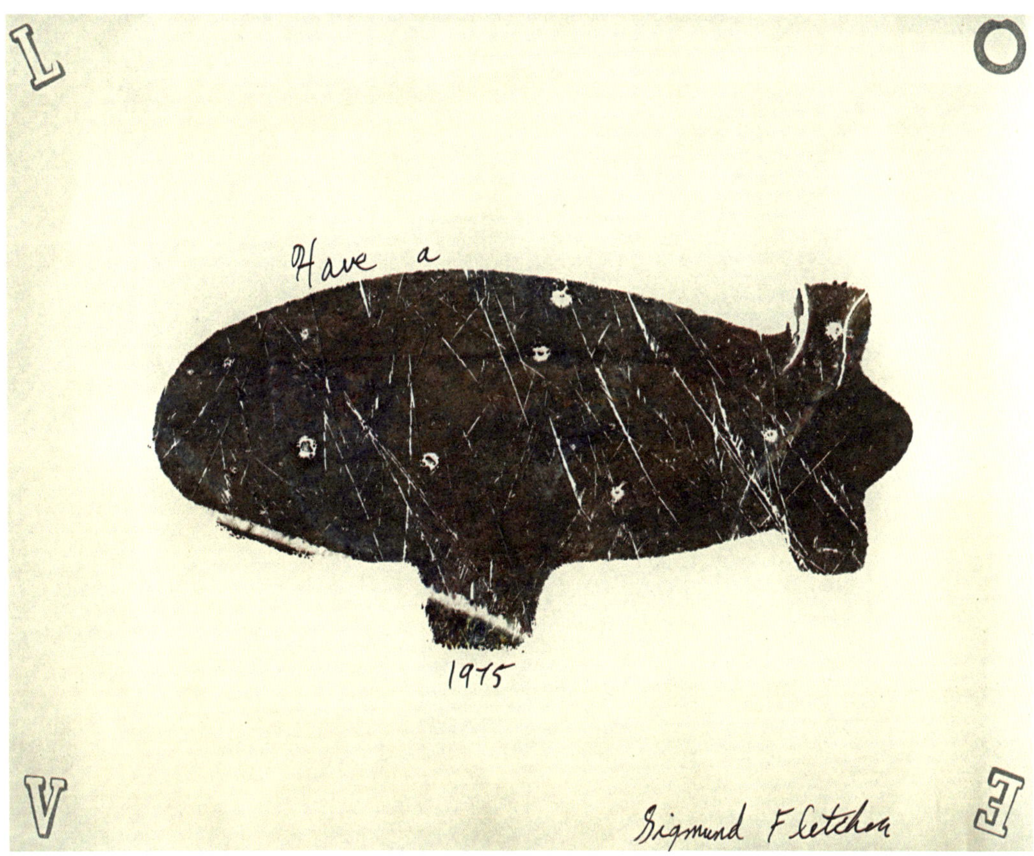

Sigmund Fletcher (Georges Herms), *Untitled*, 1975
Fondation Collection Centre PasquArt

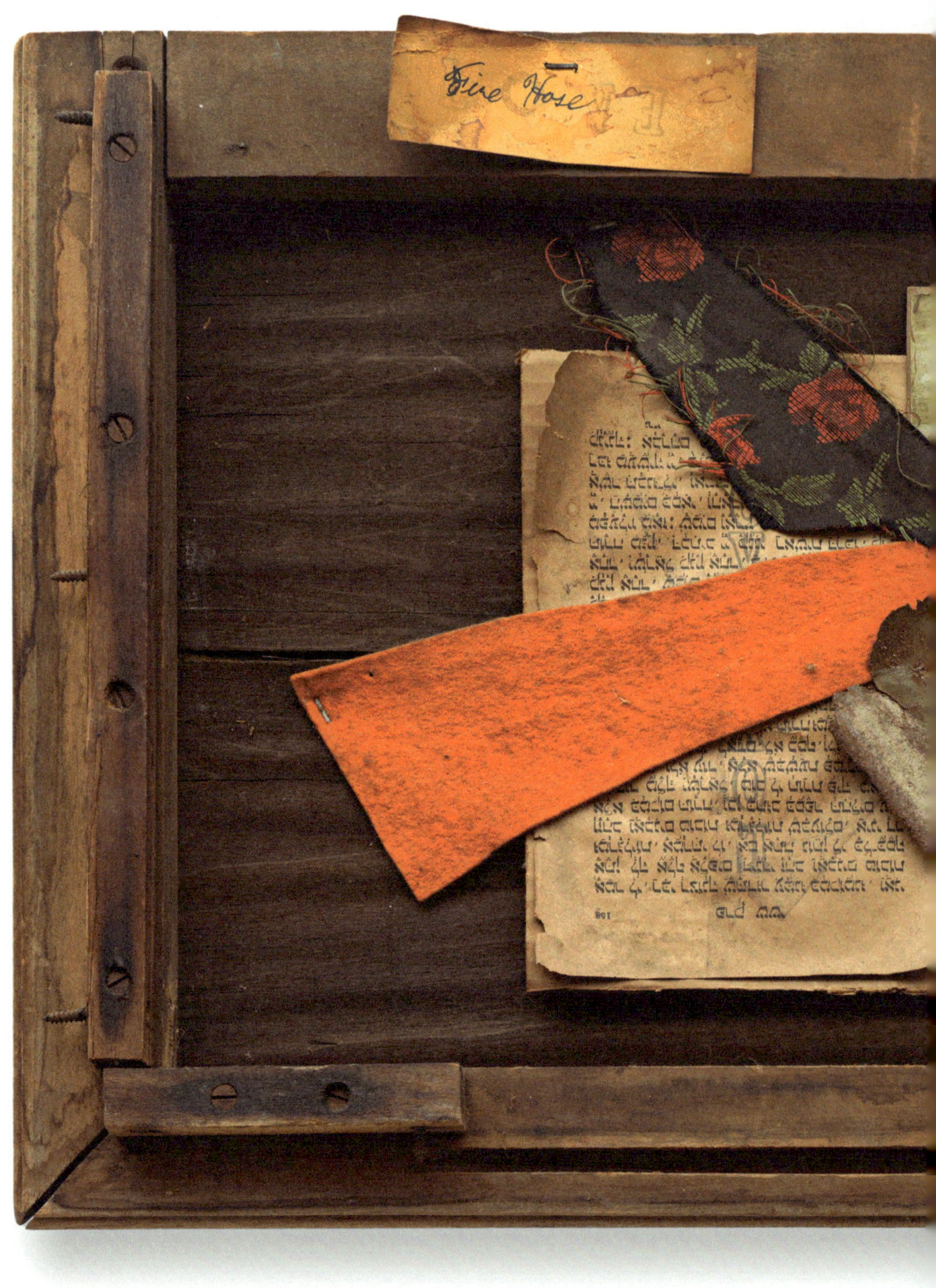

Fire Hose

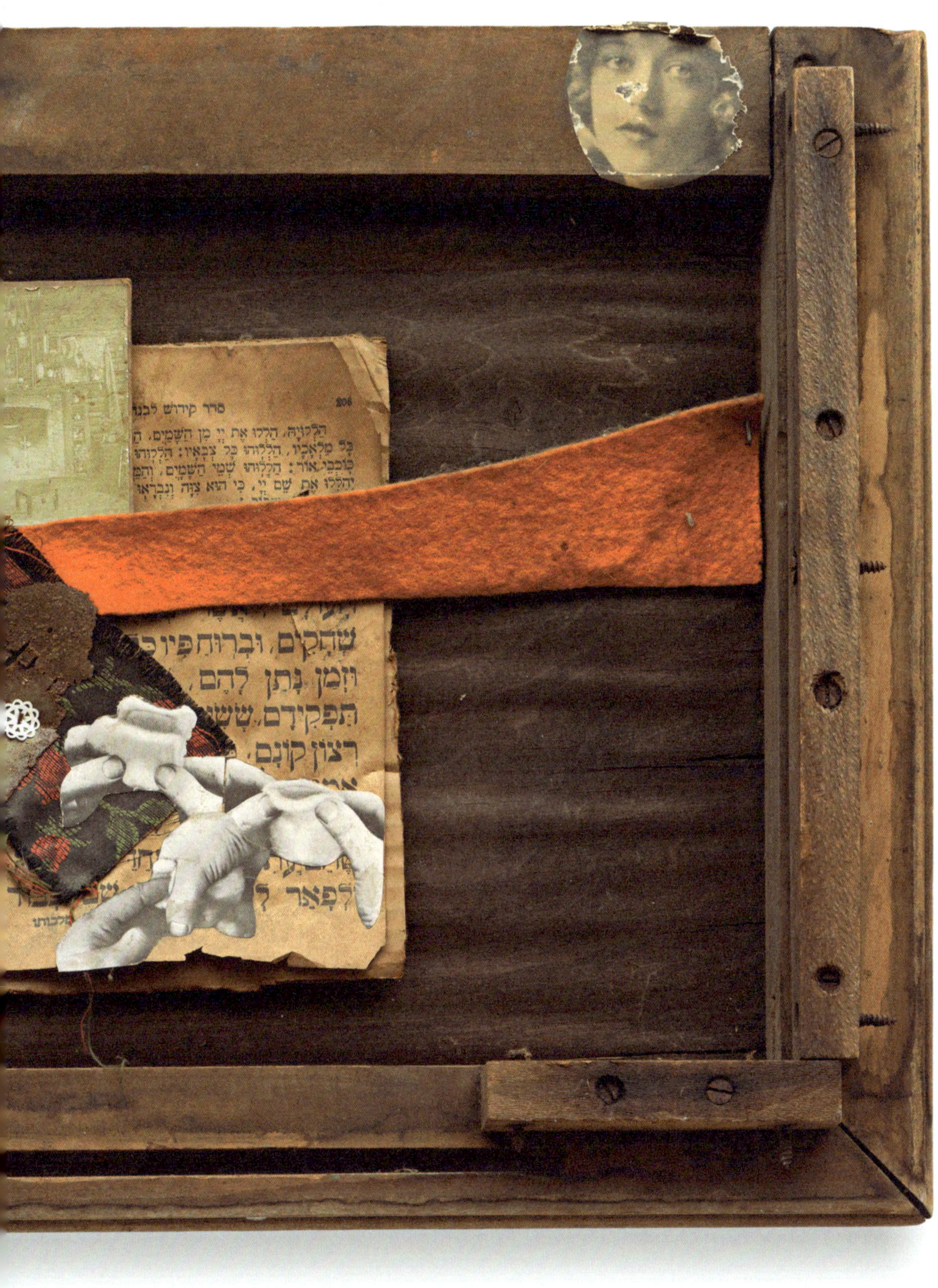

Georges Herms, *Fire Hose*, 1968
coll. MAMCO, don Mary Ann et Hal Glicksman

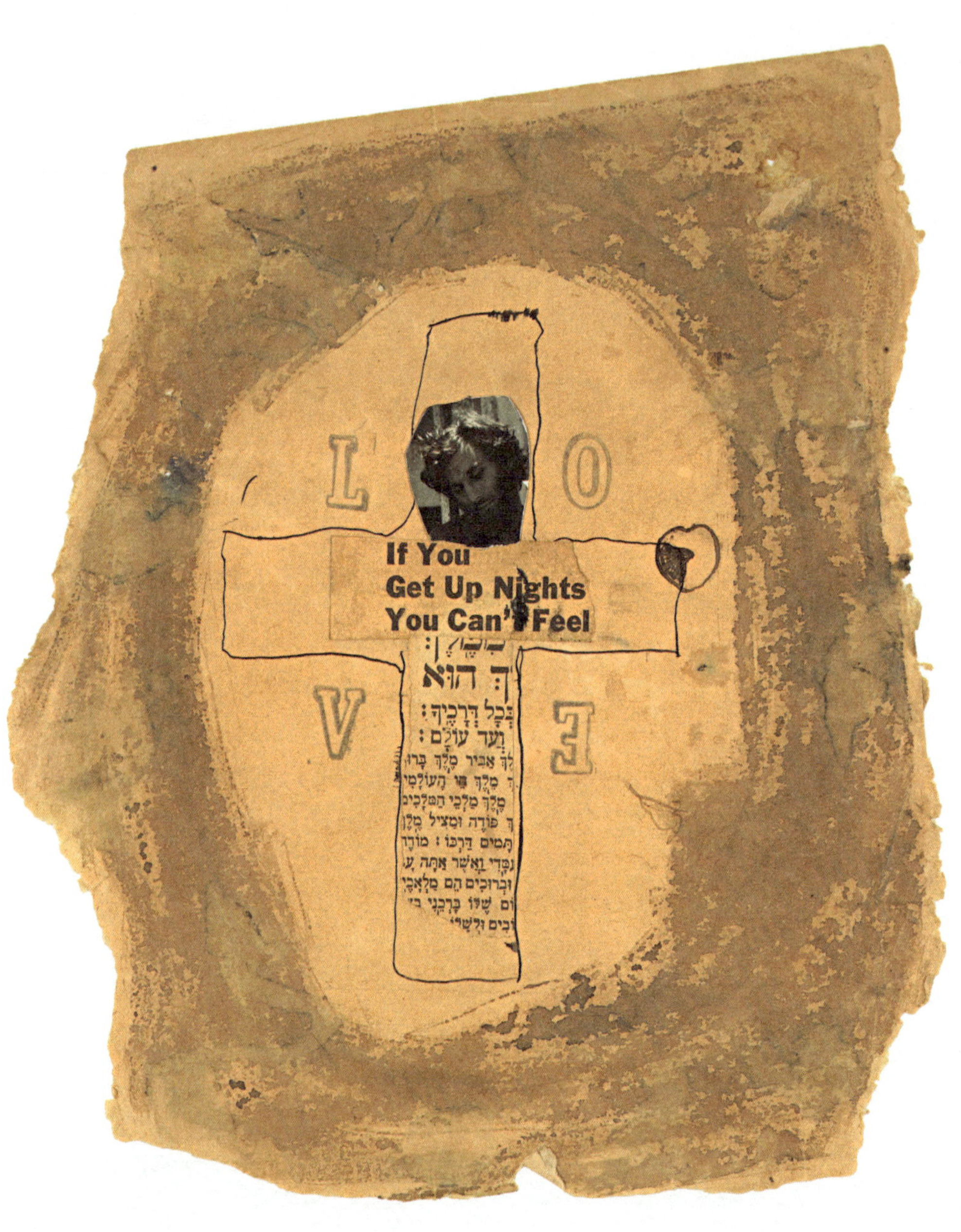

Georges Herms, *Untitled*, n.d.
Fondation Collection Centre PasquArt

began stamping the letters "L-O-V-Ǝ" on the four corners of each piece, with the backwards "E" intended to "ward off hate."[3] He has described his work as "the furniture of the soul," a reference both to his fondness for the materiality of his pieces and to common spirituality. His sculptures often take the form of altars, as if shrines to moments in a highly ritualized life—from the most everyday situations to the most fundamental encounters.

In 2006, Herms produced his *Ymeray Opera* series while staying at Hal and Mary Ann Glicksman's recently acquired farm in France ahead of a show at Galerie Vallois in Paris. He created pieces in the courtyard, garden, barns and stables, using whatever materials he could lay his hands on—old bolts, and agricultural and DIY tools. In doing so, he fashioned a series that encapsulated every facet of his work: for Herms, the farm became a larger-than-life theater. The opera's libretto, penned hastily by the artist himself and dedicated to the artist Guy de Cointet, underscored the sheer complexity of the assemblages located at different points on the property. The end result was a joyously anarchic, clattering, mechanical cabaret that bore a certain similarity to Dadaist art.

—Anne Giffon-Selle

1   G. Herms, exclusive interview with the author, 2000.
2   Sophie Dannenmüller, "George Herms, The Bricoleur of Broken Dreams," in *Herms Assemblages*, Galerie Vallois, 2006.
3   Ibid.

PAUL BEATTIE

Paul Beattie (1924–1988) enjoyed a rich and varied career that took him from New York to California, and from Abstract Expressionism to psychedelic experimentation. As a young artist, he made it his quest "to implant more of a deep space quality to Pollockian surface-patterned tracery,"[1] before ultimately leaving New York behind for the West Coast. In San Francisco, where he counted Bruce Conner and Jay DeFeo among his neighbors, he worked as a carpenter by day while focusing on his art and jazz music by night. He also contributed to the psychedelic movement by organizing projections of live-recorded films. With the support of choreographer Ann Halprin and musician Warner Jepson, he devised "live paintings," combining moving stains, figurative images and organic patterns painted on acetate.[2] He subsequently embarked on a series of sky paintings. Beattie's pieces were included in the *Collage and Assemblage in Southern California* exhibition at the Los Angeles Institute of Contemporary Art in 1975, while the San Francisco Museum of Modern Art hosted a retrospective of his work in 1980.

Turbulent Mixture (1978, ILL. P. 58–59) is part of Beattie's series of *Sky Paintings* (1975–1985). A few years earlier, Hal Glicksman had hosted *The Sky Show* at the Otis Art Gallery, featuring names including Peter Alexander, Shirley Pettibone, and Bruce Nauman. In a review of the exhibition for *Artforum*, Nancy Marmer emphasized the surprising topicality of depictions of the sky: "The heavens are no longer an unequivocal symbol for the spiritual state: 'upper air' also means sinister outer space."[3] For his drawings during this period, Beattie drew on scientific imagery of the distant and infinitesimally small, with works and series bearing names like *Early Colliding Galaxy*, *Large Graphite Planet*, *Light Filaments* and *Plasma Wave*. His pieces combined elements of gestural painting, darkness and obscurity, and discarded everyday objects. The product of an age of choking exhaust fumes and wasteful consumerist culture, *Turbulent Mixture* is a Constable-style painting devised as a tribute to an impure space of representation.

— Julien Fronsacq

1   Paul Beattie, "Summary of a Career," 22 April 1975, Beattie archive, Robyn Beattie, Petaluma. Michael Duncan and Kristine McKenna, *Semina Culture: Wallace Berman & His Circle*, Santa Monica Museum of Art, 2015, p. 84.

2   Jason Steidman, "Paul Beattie: Finally, A New Face in the Lost History of Beat Era Projection Art," 6 March 2019, at lightsweetcrude, *Listen To The Colour*: https://lightsweetcrude-music.wordpress.com/2019/03/06/paul-beattie-finally-a-new-face-in-the-lost-history-of-beat-era-projection-art/.

3   Nancy Marmer, "The Sky Show," *Artforum*, February 1976.

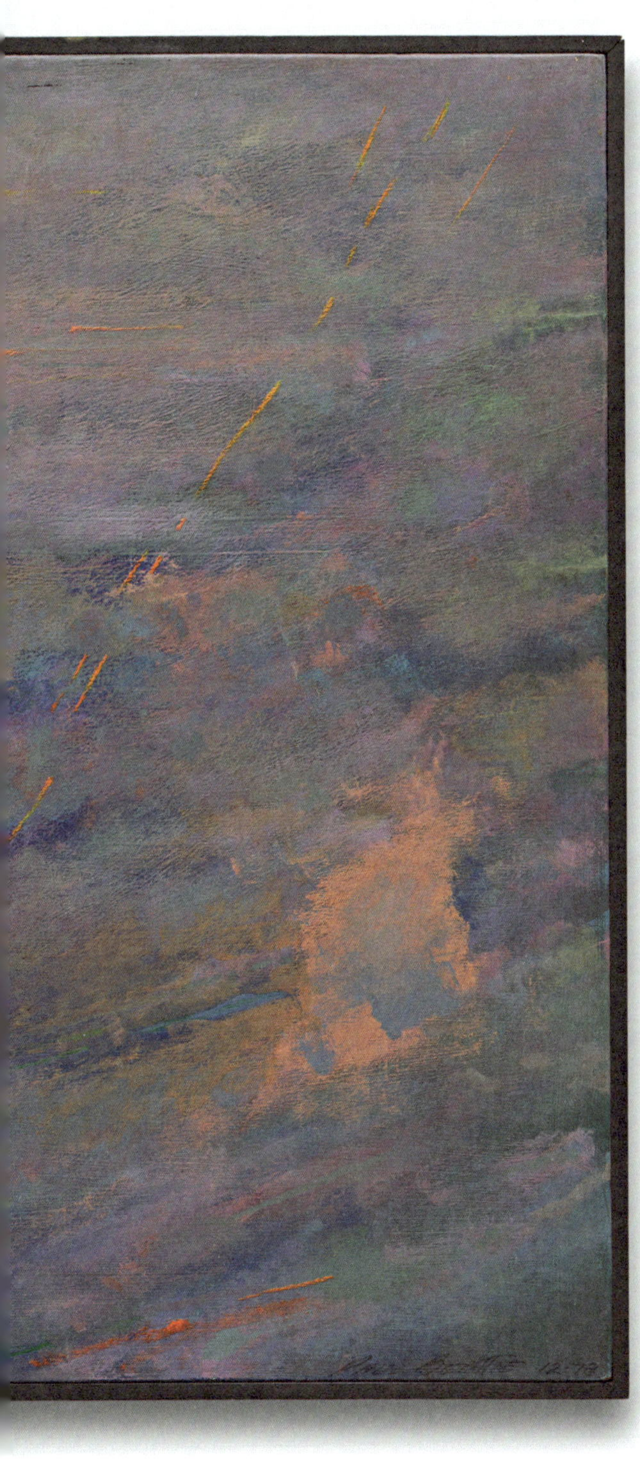

Paul Beattie, *Turbulent Mixture,* 1978
coll. MAMCO, don Mary Ann et Hal Glicksman

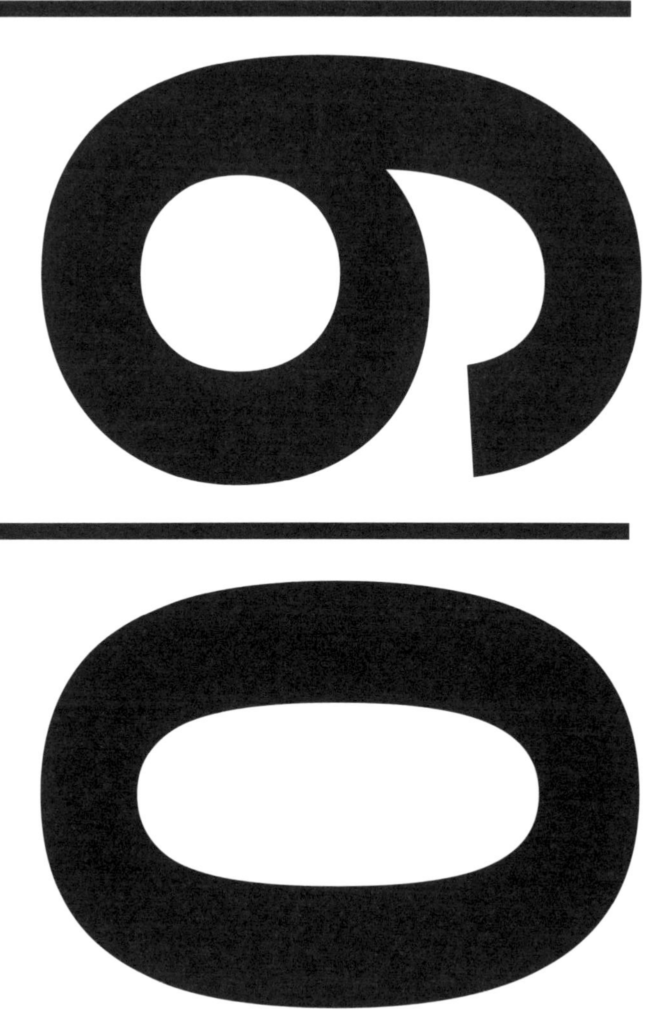

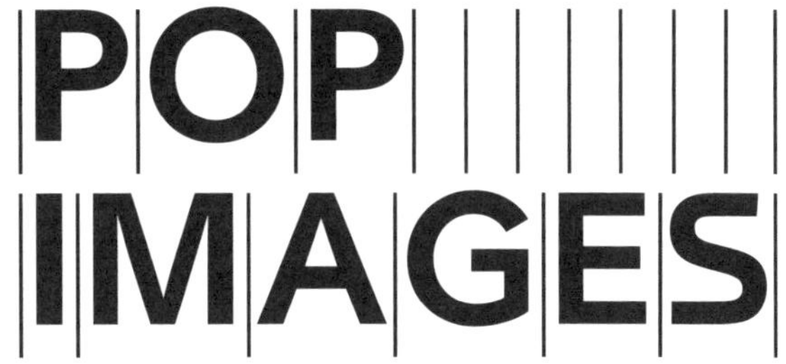

POP IMAGES

Julien Fronsacq

"The culture industry intentionally integrates its consumers from above. To the detriment of both it forces together the spheres of high and low art, separated for thousands of years."

— Theodor W. Adorno

Theodor W. Adorno fled Nazi Germany, taking his research on the culture industry with him in his satchel. He headed to Los Angeles, where he joined his compatriots Bertolt Brecht and Fritz Lang. The donations from the Glicksman collection shed light on the relationship between Californian artists and pop culture. They also testify to the sheer number of major exhibitions held in Los Angeles in the early 1960s—all curated by Walter Hopps—focusing on the intersection between the arts and consumerism.

In 1962, as MoMA in New York held the *Pop Art Symposium*, Andy Warhol showed his *Campbell's Soup Cans* at the Ferus Gallery—the same venue where Edward Kienholz would later come to prominence for his passé yet disconcerting depictions of everyday environments. That same year, the Pasadena Art Museum played host to an exhibition of paintings of common objects, including works by New York Pop exponents and several young Californian artists (Phillip Hefferton, Edward Ruscha, and Wayne Thiebaud).[1] A separate retrospective featured a selection of "Merz" collages by Kurt Schwitters.[2] In 1963, Glicksman met Hopps during a retrospective of the works of Marcel Duchamp at the same Pasadena venue. As a young student living in Venice Beach, Glicksman witnessed the Beat Generation firsthand and came into contact with artists such as Ben Talbert and Fred Mason. He also developed an interest in the work of George Herms, Wallace Berman, and Bruce Conner from the San Francisco scene. In 1968, Glicksman co-curated an exhibition of Californian Assemblage with Hopps and John Coplans, helping the movement gain recognition among traditional art circles.

Stuart Perkoff's *Untitled* (1959, ILL. P. 63) attests to the importance of literature to the Beat Generation[3]: the collage uses

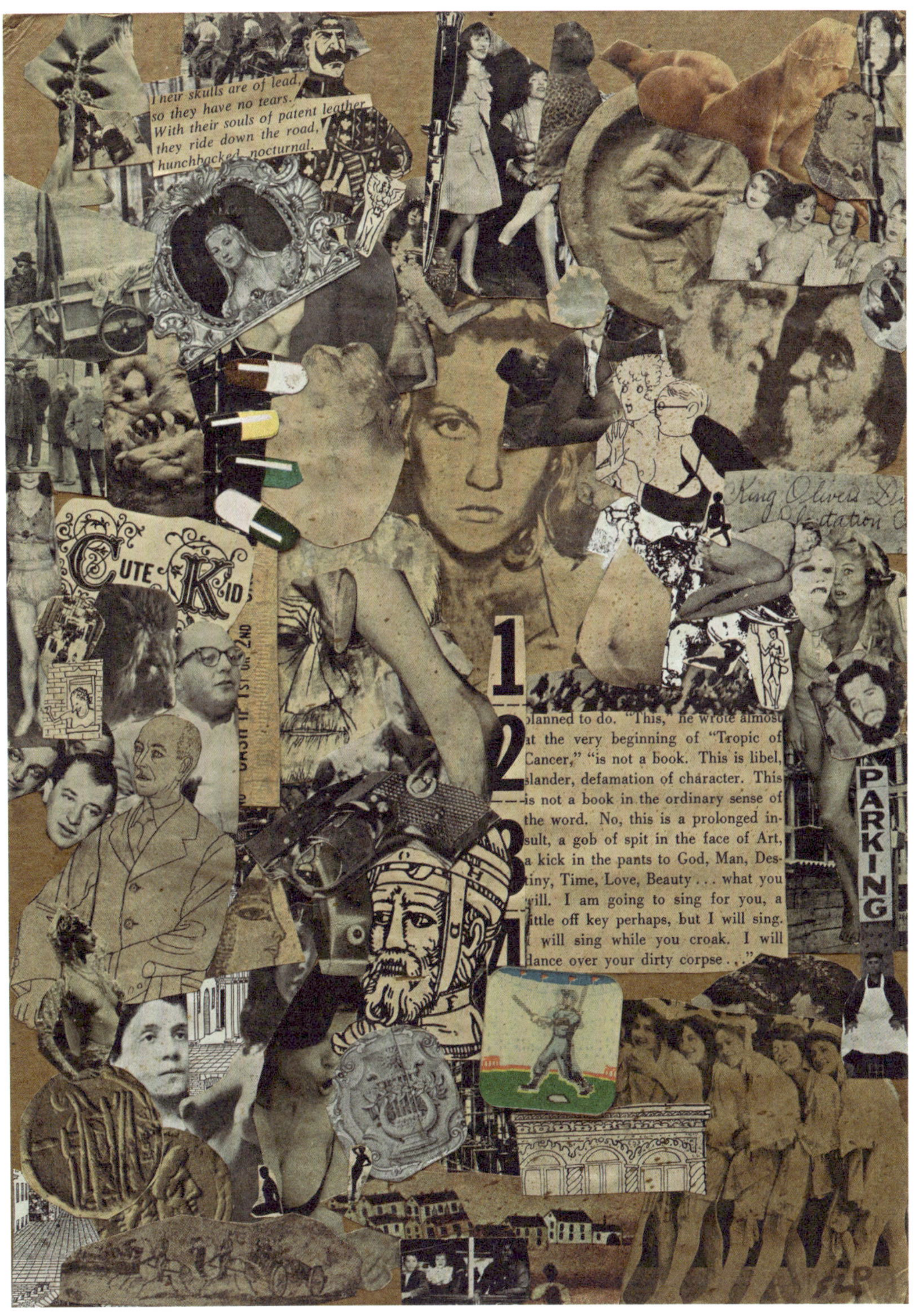

Stuart Perkoff, *Untitled ("Their Skulls are of Lead")*, 1959
coll. MAMCO, don Mary Ann et Hal Glicksman

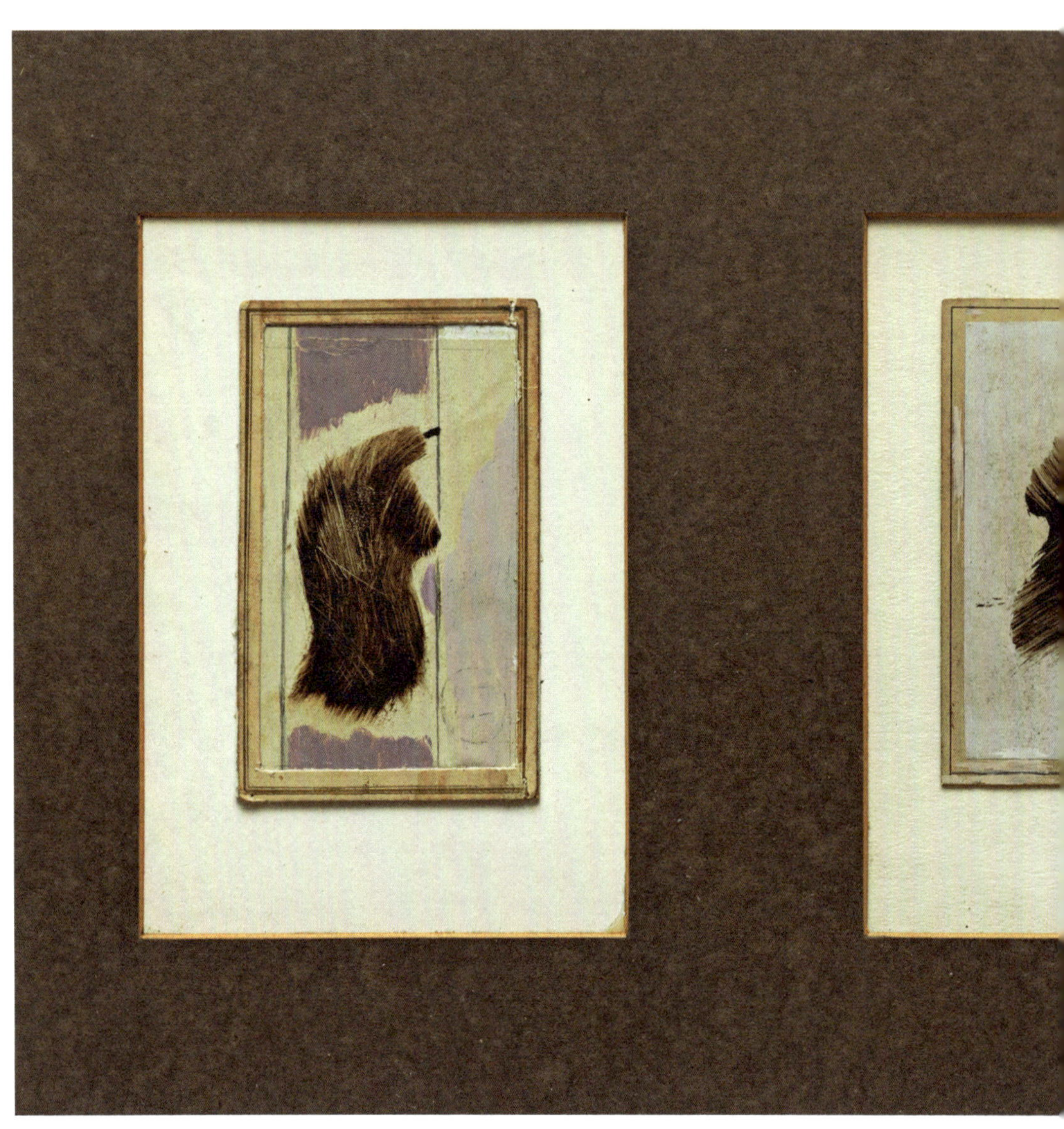

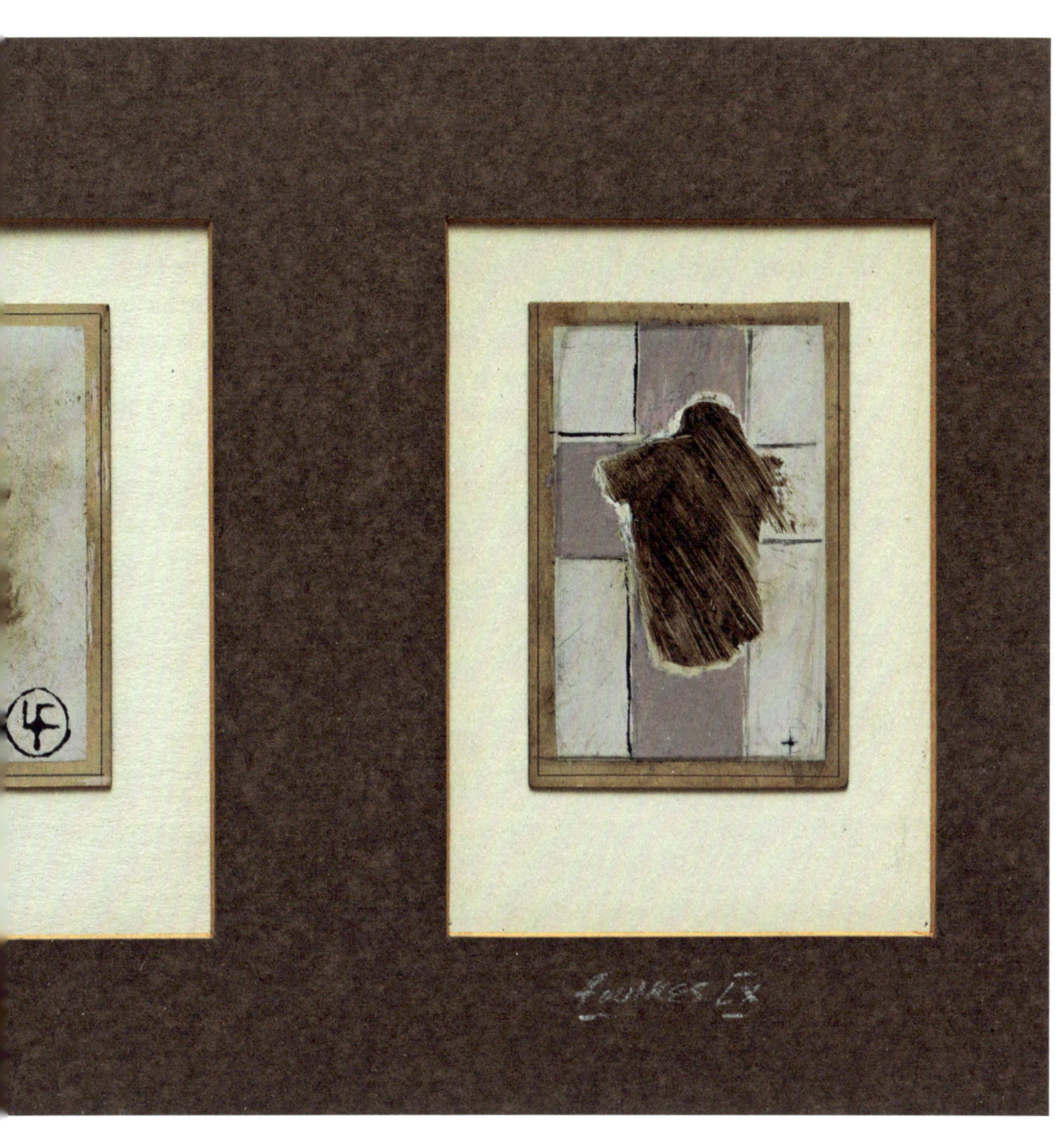

Llyn Foulkes, *Untitled,* circa 1960
coll. MAMCO, don Mary Ann et Hal Glicksman

recycled images and excerpts from writings by Federico García Lorca and Henry Miller, giving the piece an anarchic and iconoclastic character.

Many of the donated works also testify to the critical stance against U.S. policy at the height of the Cold War adopted by Hefferton, Herms, and Talbert. Herms' *Untitled (How To Carry The Injured)* consists of an A-shaped advertising board (of the kind found on sidewalks outside stores) adorned with an American flag and a photograph of scouts engaged in a training exercise [ILL. P. 67]. Hefferton, meanwhile, made use of the dollar sign and other, related symbols of power: in one example, a dollar bill appears on a textured, chocolate-colored background, as if the currency were associated with excrement [ILL. P. 72–73]; in another, a nickel is depicted as a bomb being released by a bomber [ILL. P. 71).

1 The exhibition, entitled *New Painting of Common Objects* and curated by Hopps, took place in 1962, one year before Lawrence Alloway's show at the Guggenheim Museum in New York. The poster is held in the collection of the Kunsthaus Pasquart in Biel/Bienne.

2 "Merz" is a word invented by Schwitters in 1919 to describe his collage and assemblage works. It comes from the second syllable of the German word Kommerz (commerce). See Benjamin Buchloh, "Faktura et factographie" (1984), in *Essais historiques, t.I: Art moderne*, Villeurbanne, Art édition, coll. Textes, 1992.

3 See the article by Anne Giffon-Selle here, as well as her book *Les astronautes du dedans* (MAMCO and Les presses du réel, 2017).

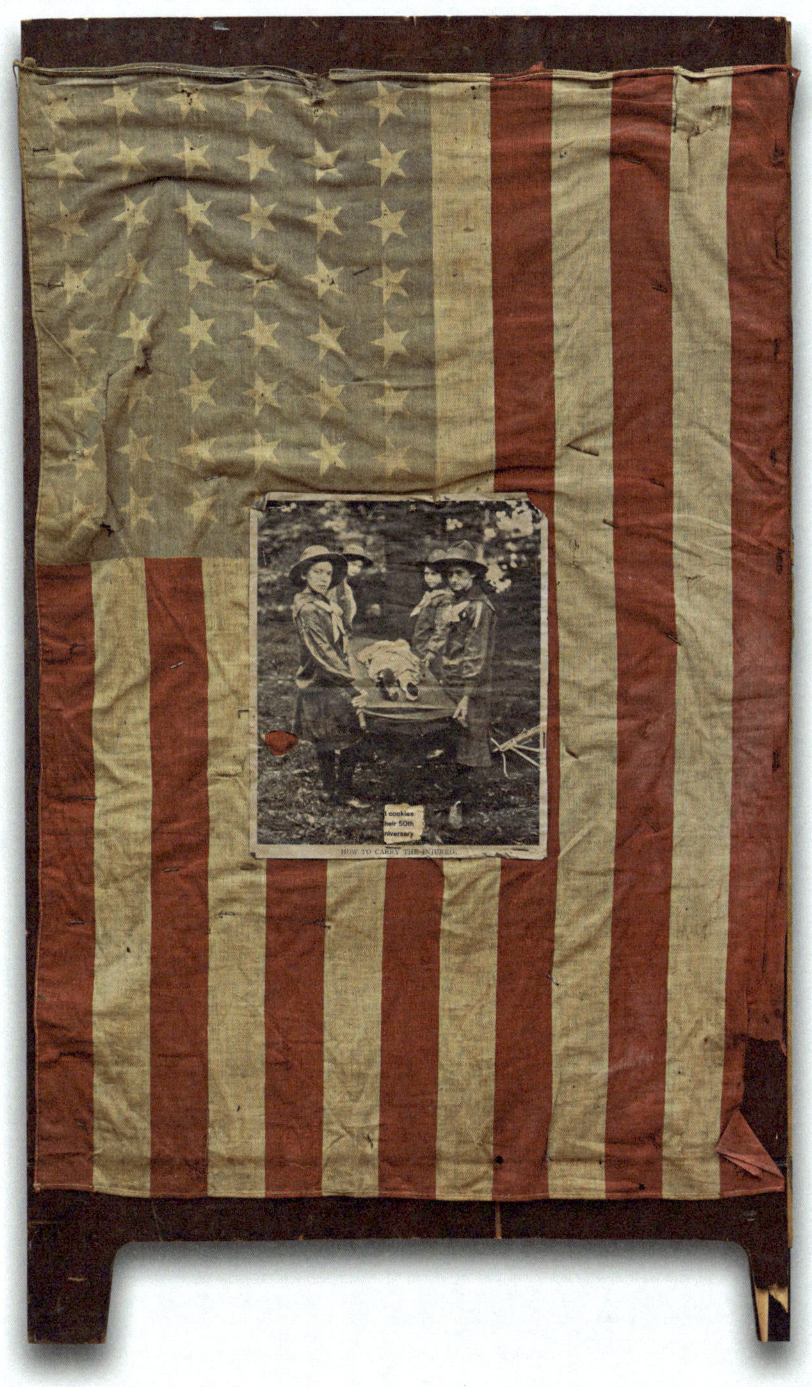

George Herms, *Untitled (How To Carrie The Injured)*, n.d.
coll. MAMCO, don Mary Ann et Hal Glicksman

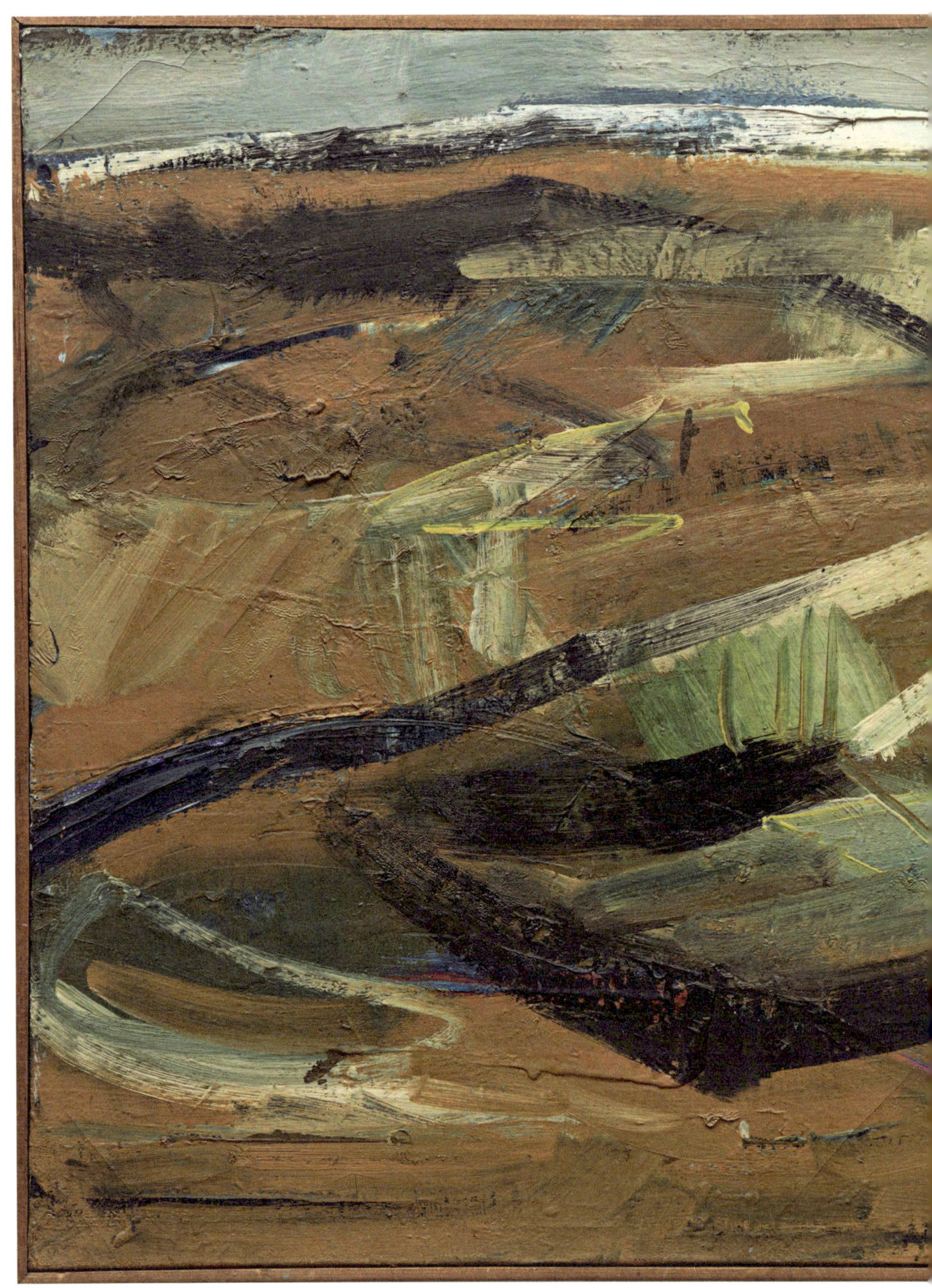

Billy Al Bengston, *Road Runner*, 1958
coll. MAMCO, don Mary Ann et Hal Glicksman

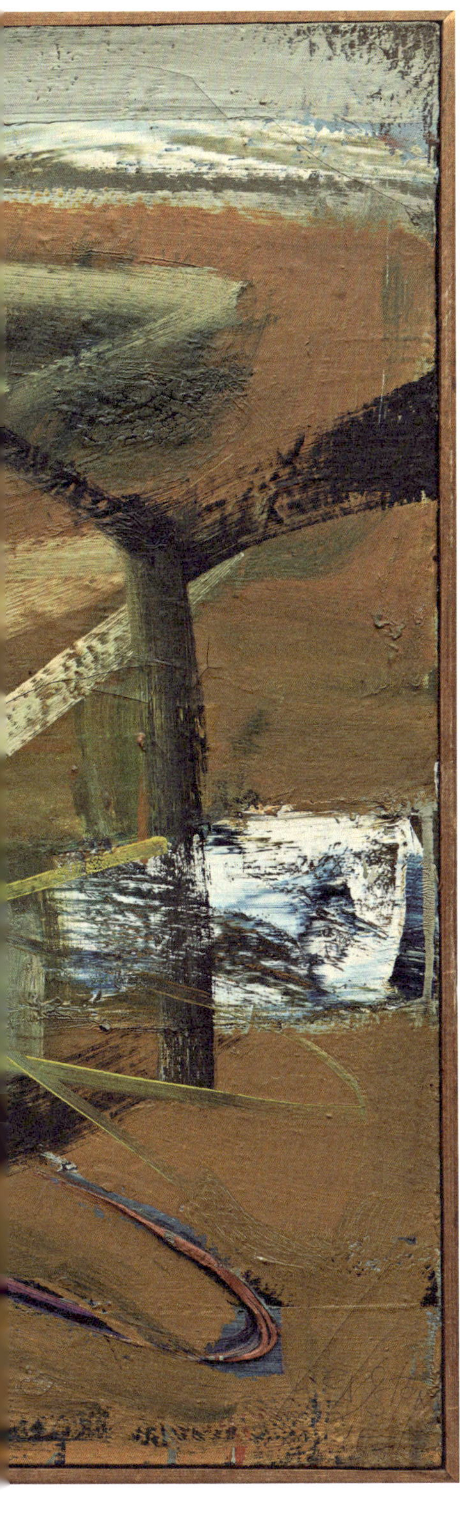

PHILLIP HEFFERTON

New Painting of Common Objects was the first Pop art exhibition to be hosted at a museum in the United States. It featured works by figures from the East Coast scene (Andy Warhol, Roy Liechtenstein, Jim Dine), young Californian artists (Ed Ruscha, Joe Goode, Wayne Thiebaud), as well as Robert Dowd and Phillip Hefferton, both of whom had recently moved to California from Detroit. The event took place a few weeks after Warhol had exhibited a *Campbell's Soup Cans* series in a solo show at the Ferus Gallery in Los Angeles. Explaining his choice of subject, Warhol said: "I used to drink it. I used to have the same lunch every day for 20 years." The choice of low-grade subject matter—a cheap can of soup—and the monotonous, repetitive pattern were particular features of American Pop art. These characteristics set it apart from British Pop art, which Lawrence Alloway and Richard Hamilton described as "sexy" and "glamorous."

In his early paintings, Hefferton (1933–2008) exclusively depicted fragments of U.S. banknotes—the same subject adopted by his friend Dowd and, later, by Warhol. Hefferton focused in particular on the portraits of Washington, Lincoln and Jackson appearing on the 1-, 5-, and 20-dollar bills, reframing and subverting the images to make the former presidents' eyes blink, inserting portraits of his own family members in their place, or replacing the signature of the Secretary of the Treasury with those of his friends (including Walter Hopps and William Copley). In one case, he depicted a small-denomination coin as a bomber [ILL. P. 71].

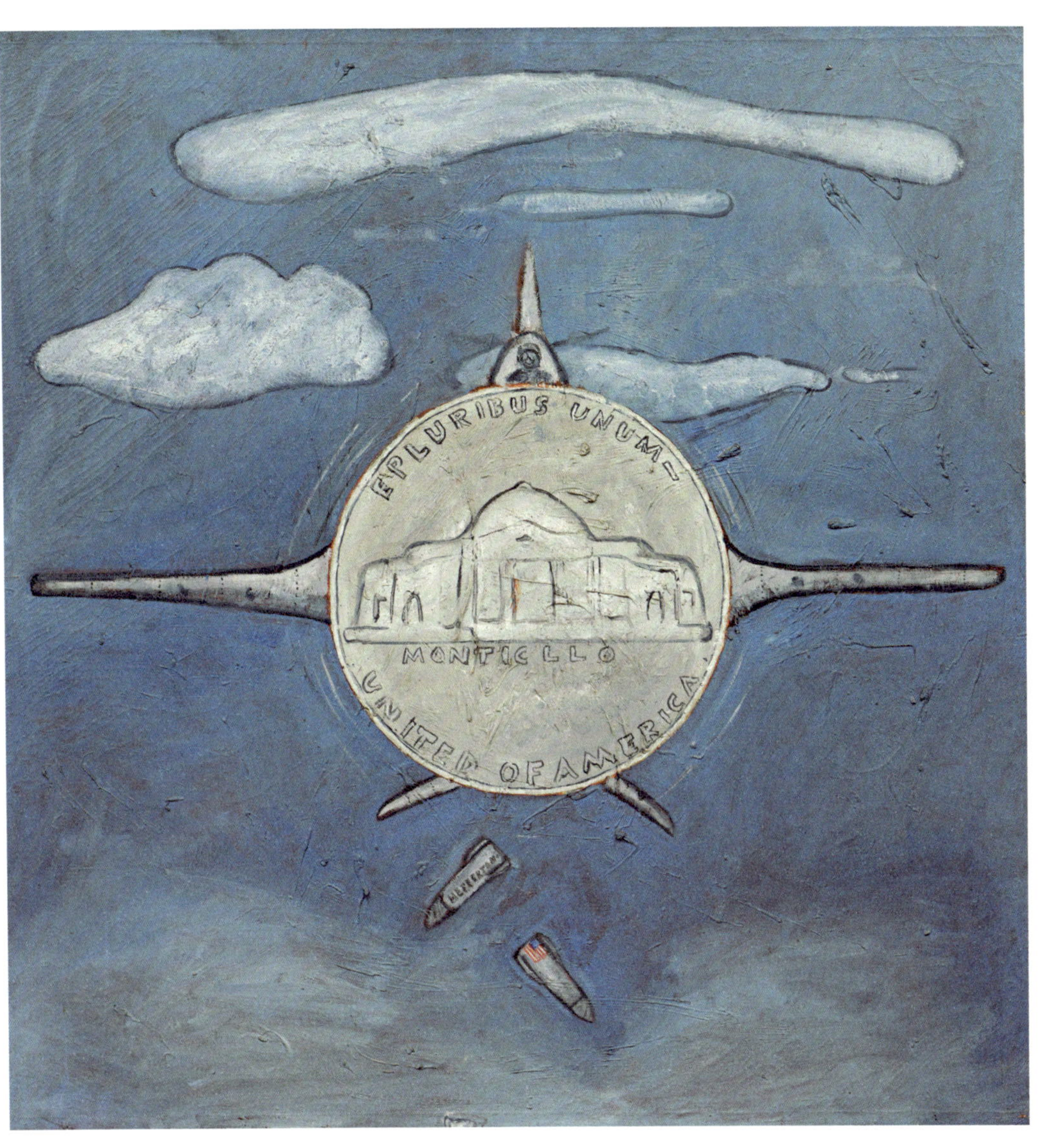

Phillip Hefferton, *Untitled,* circa 1962
coll. MAMCO, don Mary Ann et Hal Glicksman

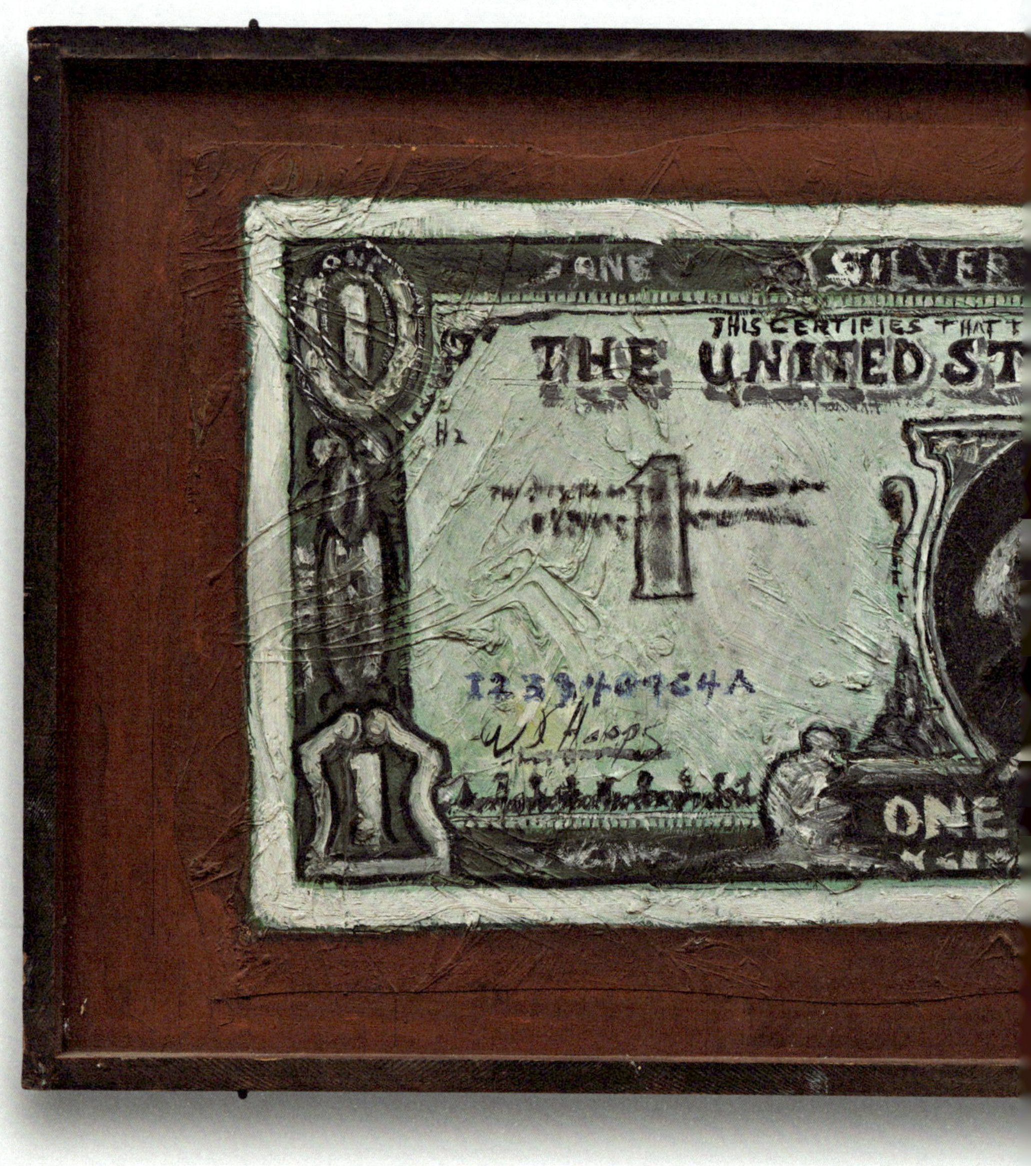

ONE
SILVER
THIS CERTIFIES THAT T
THE UNITED ST
1
ONE

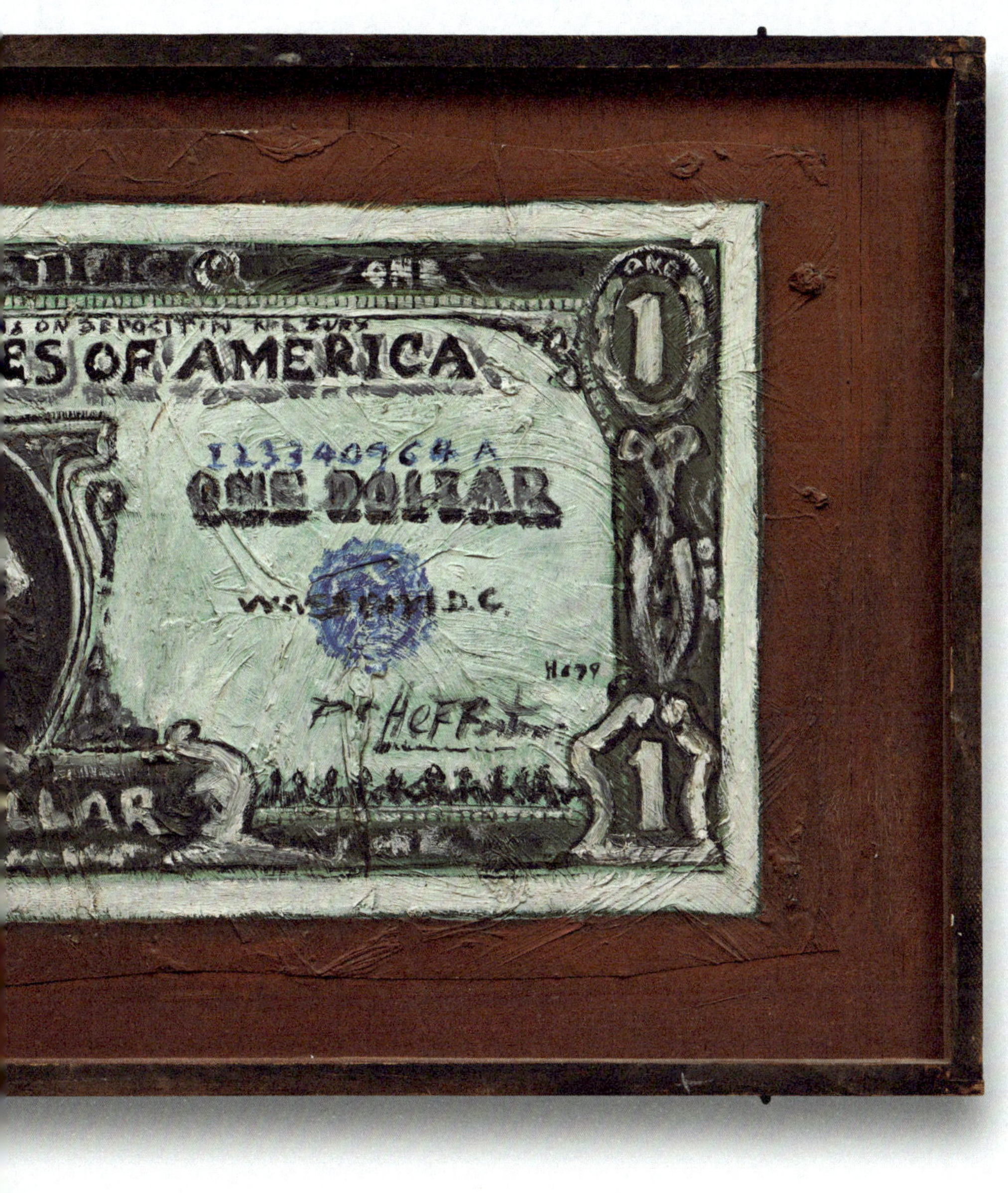

Phillip Hefferton, *Untitled*, circa 1962
coll. MAMCO, don Mary Ann et Hal Glicksman

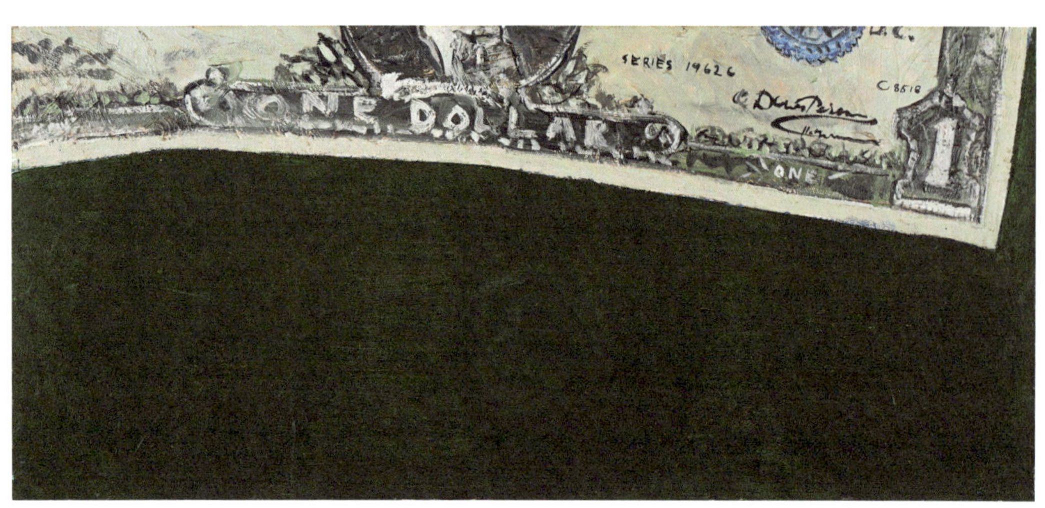

Phillip Hefferton, *Untitled,* circa 1962
Fondation Collection Centre PasquArt

Hefferton's Dadaist-style playfulness and the often-coarse execution of his paintings suggest a certain indifference toward his subject, as if the U.S. dollar and its associated mythology merit nothing more than ridicule. In hindsight, these satirical paintings seem to capture the mood of their day—one reflected in both the visual arts and music. That is what art critic John Coplans appeared to imply in his review of *New Painting of Common Objects* for *Artforum*: "The proverbial dumbness of most younger artists on the West Coast, for example, is a reflection not only of their deep understanding of the lie of the evolution of progress, but also an affirmation of the basis of both Jazz and Beat poetry, that art springs directly from life, with all its anguish."

— Paul Bernard

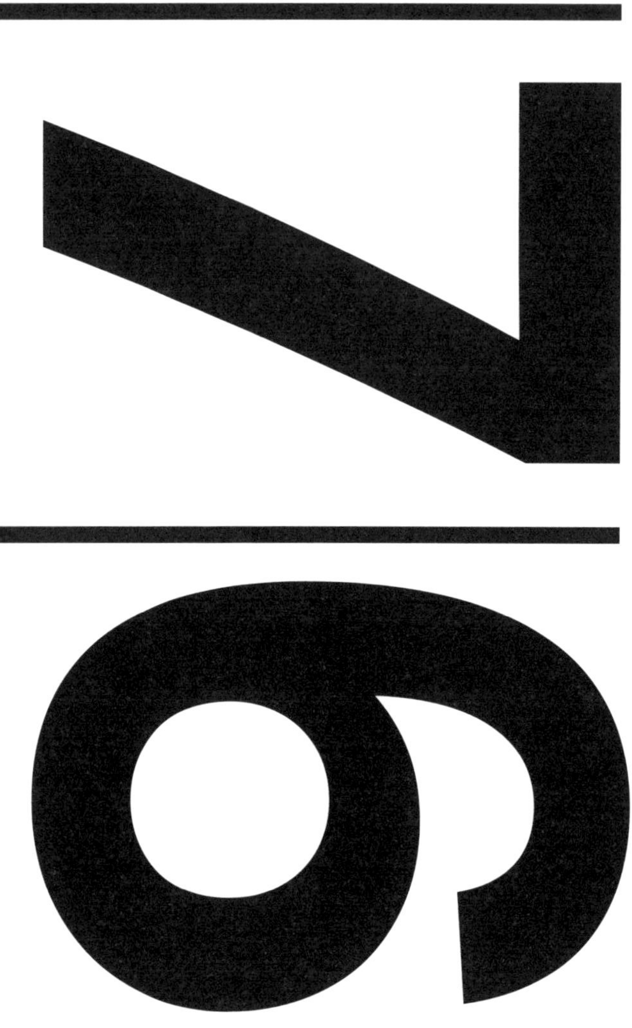

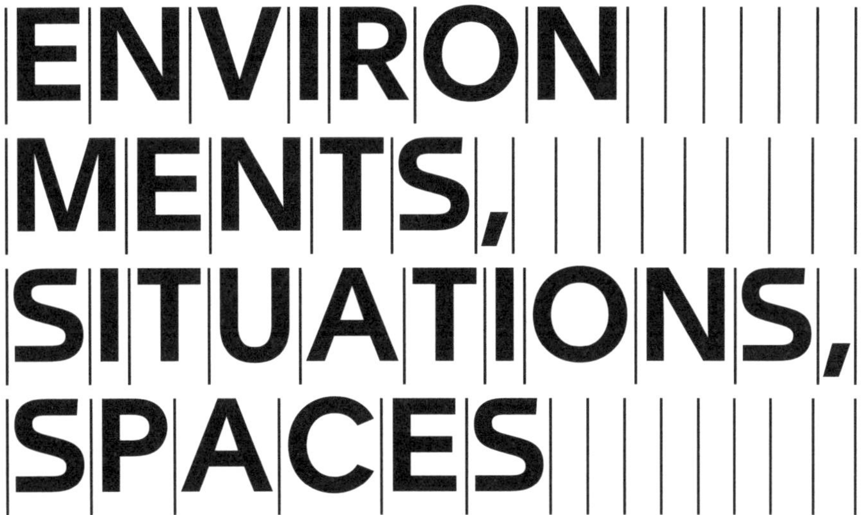

ENVIRONMENTS, SITUATIONS, SPACES

Julien Fronsacq

In 1970, MoMA in New York hosted *Spaces*, an exhibition that touched on concepts of space, architecture and the role of museums as arenas for artistic production.[1] In the same year, Hal Glicksman began using his position as a curator to take a fresh look at the notion of installations, inviting several artists to design settings for a number of his shows.

Michael Asher, who had recently produced an acoustic installation using the architecture at the La Jolla Museum of Art [ILL. P. 79], brought his sensory and institutional deconstructivist approach to the Pomona College Museum of Art: a wall was erected through the gallery and two doors were left open around the clock, creating a vacuum environment that served as a "wind tunnel" [ILL. P. 117]. A few weeks later, Judy Chicago produced an outdoor installation on Mount Baldy above Pomona, transforming the landscape with clouds of white smoke (*Snow Atmosphere*). In May of the same year, Tom Eatherton unveiled *Rise*, a semicircular diorama with complex lighting that transformed the viewer's perception of space, procuring the "eerie sensation" of "walking in the floor, up to [one's] knees."[2]

In 1972, Glicksman took up the role of director of the art center at UC Irvine. There, he curated a number of site-specific projects, including works by Larry Bell, Peter Alexander, and Jane Reynolds, as well as a Bruce Nauman *Floating Room*: a hanging cube with no anchor points, just like the letters in the poster designed by the artist [ILL. P. 111]. That same year, for her installation *Saddleback Mountain*, Maria Nordman completely transformed the gallery space, creating a high, narrow entrance opening out onto a mirror[3] [ILL. P. 112–113].

The donated works include other references to this process of spatial experimentation: unfinished in situ projects by Asher from Glicksman's time at the Corcoran Gallery of Art in Washington, D.C. [ILL. P. 118]; a sketch of a row of ladders entitled *Land of Lads* accompanied by the mysterious words "A half ladder is better than a(ny) ladder at all," as a memento of Rosemarie Castoro's show at the Otis Art Gallery [ILL. P. 79]; and a mural by Sol LeWitt, one

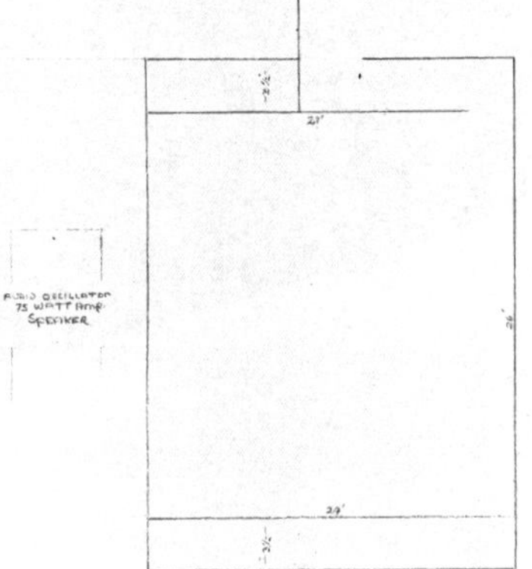

Michael Asher, *Final Work for La Jolla Art Museum*, Meyer Gallery, 1969
coll. MAMCO, don Mary Ann et Hal Glicksman
Rosemarie Castoro, *Untitled*, 1976
coll. MAMCO, don Mary Ann et Hal Glicksman

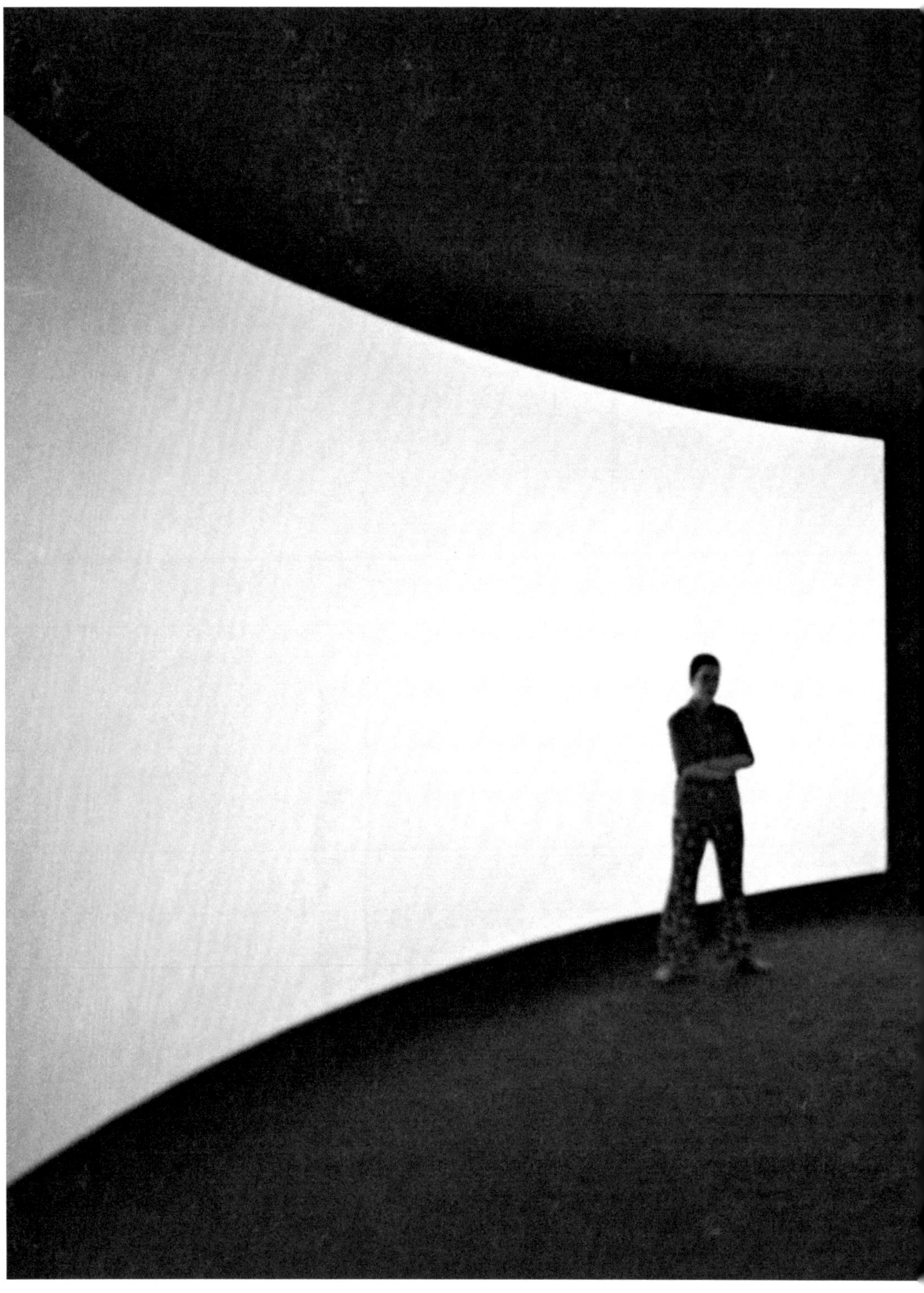

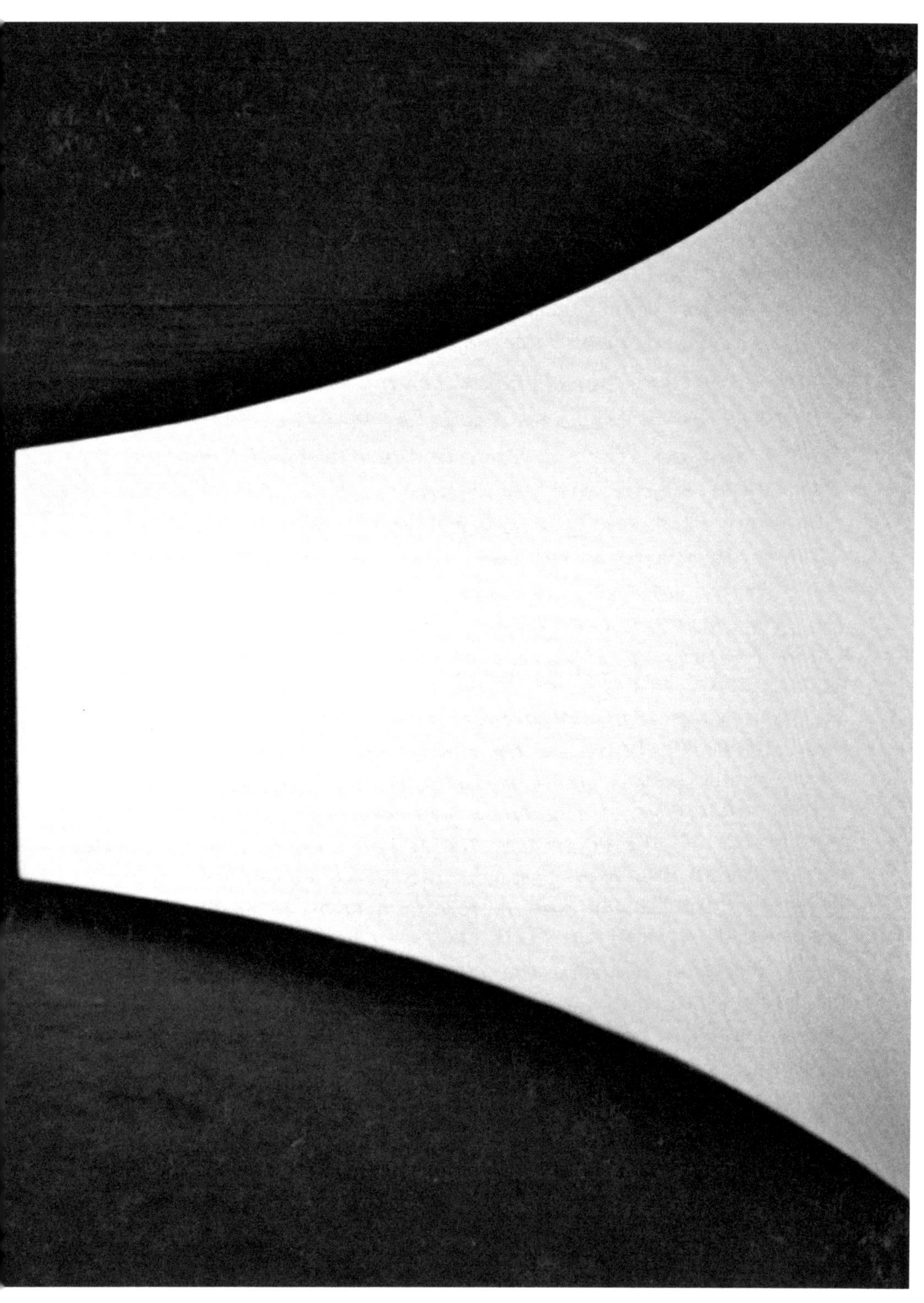

Tom Eatherton, *Rise*, Pomona College Museum of Art, 1970
Don Hal Glicksman. Getty Research Institute, Los Angeles (2009.M.5)

A CIRCLE WHOSE RADIUS IS EQUAL TO HALF THE DISTANCE BETWEEN TWO POINTS, THE FIRST POINT IS FOUND WHERE TWO LINES WOULD CROSS IF THE FIRST LINE ~~OF THE FIRST SET~~ WERE DRAWN FROM A POINT HALFWAY BETWEEN A POINT HALFWAY BETWEEN THE CENTER OF THE WALL AND THE UPPER LEFT CORNER AND THE MID-POINT OF THE TOP SIDE TO A POINT HALFWAY BETWEEN THE CENTER OF THE WALL AND THE MIDPOINT OF THE LEFT SIDE AND A POINT HALFWAY BETWEEN THE MIDPOINT OF THE LEFT SIDE AND THE LOWER LEFT CORNER, THE SECOND LINE ~~OF THE FIRST SET~~ IF IT WERE DRAWN FROM A POINT HALFWAY BETWEEN ~~THE~~ A POINT HALFWAY BETWEEN THE CENTER OF THE WALL AND A POINT HALFWAY BETWEEN ~~THE CENTER OF THE WALL AND A POINT HALFWAY BETWEEN~~ THE MIDPOINT OF THE RIGHT SIDE AND THE UPPER RIGHT CORNER AND THE MIDPOINT OF THE RIGHT SIDE TO A POINT HALFWAY BETWEEN A POINT HALFWAY BETWEEN ~~A POINT~~ THE CENTER OF THE WALL AND THE UPPER LEFT CORNER AND A POINT HALFWAY BETWEEN THE MIDPOINT OF THE LEFT SIDE AND THE UPPER LEFT CORNER; THE SECOND POINT IS FOUND WHERE TWO ~~SETS OF~~ LINES WOULD CROSS IF THE FIRST LINE WERE DRAWN FROM A POINT HALFWAY BETWEEN A POINT HALFWAY BETWEEN THE CENTER OF THE WALL AND THE MIDPOINT OF THE BOTTOM SIDE AND A POINT HALFWAY BETWEEN THE CENTER OF THE WALL AND THE LOWER RIGHT CORNER TO A POINT HALFWAY BETWEEN THE END OF THE FIRST LINE OF THE FIRST SET AND THE END OF THE SECOND LINE OF THE FIRST SET, THE SECOND LINE IF IT WERE DRAWN FROM A POINT HALFWAY BETWEEN THE POINT WHERE THE FIRST TWO LINES HAVE CROSSED AND A POINT HALFWAY BETWEEN THE STARTING ~~POINT~~ OF THE FIRST LINE OF THE FIRST SET AND A POINT HALFWAY BETWEEN THE MIDPOINT OF THE RIGHT SIDE AND THE UPPER RIGHT CORNER TO A POINT HALFWAY BETWEEN THE END OF THE FIRST LINE OF THE SECOND SET AND A POINT HALF-WAY BETWEEN THE CENTER OF THE WALL AND THE MIDPOINT OF THE BOTTOM SIDE; AND WHOSE CENTER IS LOCATED EQUIDISTANT TO THREE POINTS, THE FIRST OF WHICH IS LOCATED

AT THE CENTER OF THE WALL, THE SECOND POINT IS LOCATED
AT A POINT HALFWAY BETWEEN A POINT HALFWAY BETWEEN
THE CENTER OF THE WALL AND THE UPPER RIGHT CORNER AND
A POINT HALFWAY BETWEEN THE CENTER OF THE WALL AND
A POINT HALFWAY BETWEEN THE MIDPOINT OF THE RIGHT
SIDE AND THE UPPER RIGHT CORNER, THE THIRD POINT IS
LOCATED HALFWAY BETWEEN THE STARTING POINT OF THE FIRST
LINE OF THE FIRST SET AND THE END OF THE FIRST LINE
OF THE SECOND SET.

PROPOSAL FOR WALL DRAWING AT UNIV. OF CALIF.
AT IRVINE. MARCH 13, 1974. SOL LEWITT

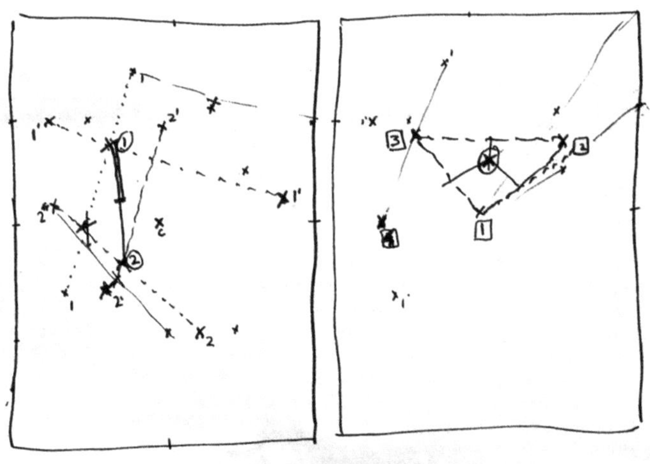

FOR HAL / MARCH 13, 1974 / Sol Lewitt

Sol LeWitt, *Untitled (Proposal for Wall Drawing at University of California, Irvine)*, 1974
coll. MAMCO, don Mary Ann et Hal Glicksman

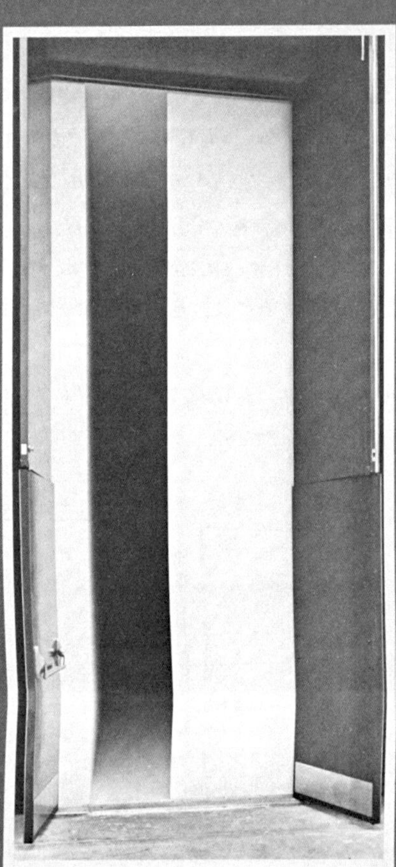

Maria Nordman, exhibition poster *Saddleback Mountain*, University of California, Irvine, 1973
coll. MAMCO, don Mary Ann et Hal Glicksman

of only a handful of items in the donated collection that can be re-exhibited [ILL. P. 82–83].

Writing about this Californian trend for pared-back installations, art critic Germano Celant emphasized the depth of experience they offered: "These spaces (...) being permeated with emptiness and nothing-ness, immobility and non-images, do in fact bring on a state of concentration and inward meditation. They seem to take one into non-matter, but this sensation turns out to be 'full of things.'"[4]

1   Press release, *Spaces*, MoMA, 30 December 1969 to 1 March 1970.

2   Peter Plagens, *Artforum*, September 1970: "I had the eerie sensation I was walking in the floor, up to my knees. The world in *Rise* is singular, with no extraneous objects and no outside sensations disturbing its purity."

3   Peter Plagens, "Maria Nordman," *Artforum*, February 1974.

4   Germano Celant, "Arte Ambientale Californiana," in *Domus*, No. 547, June 1975; translated from *Italian in Painting and Sculpture in California: The Modern Era*, San Francisco Museum of Modern Art, 1977.

MARIA NORDMAN

For her early works, Maria Nordman (born in 1943 in Görlitz, Germany; lives in Los Angeles) filmed scenes from everyday life such as eating and smoking; transformed desert landscapes using fire and smoke; and created inventories of abandoned buildings. These pieces, which stand at the intersection of landscape and performance art, were baptized "photo-fragments"—a name that captures the limits inherent in this kind of technical description. The relationship between architecture and its social and environmental context is a theme that runs throughout Nordman's body of work, produced over a career that began in the late 1960s and spanned half a century. One of her first physical installations, titled *Moveable Walls* (1969), consisted of a series of black walls that could be moved around the studio to harness the effects of natural light and shade. After producing *Saddleback Mountain* [ILL. P. 112–113] for UC Irvine in 1973, she created a series of in situ installations that brought the outside world into the museum space. For the *documenta 6* exhibition, she chose a store with a window as the setting for a structure with two entrances—a hybrid between outdoors and indoors. In 1989, she constructed a house at the edge of New York's Central Park, where the park's greenery met the city's streets. The building, which was open to the public, had two rooms: one where people could spend a few moments during the daytime, and a second where passing strangers could spend the night. Designed to be dismantled and moved, the structure was transferred to MAMCO when it opened in 1994. Since then, it has been displayed as separate parts illuminated by the soft glow of oil lamps or, as the artist herself said, "in a state where each of its parts is a potential sculpture." The museum acquired this (untitled) work in 2017 [ILL. P. 87–89].

—Julien Fronsacq

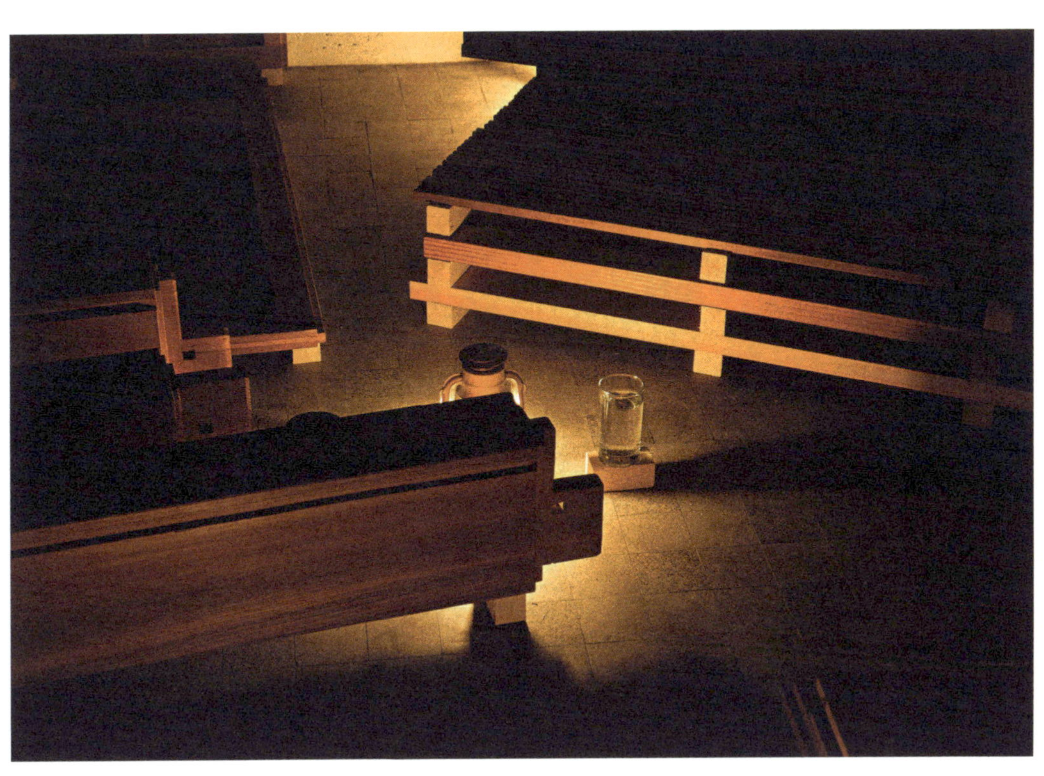

Maria Nordman, *Untitled, 1989-...*, 1989
coll. MAMCO, don Pierre Darier

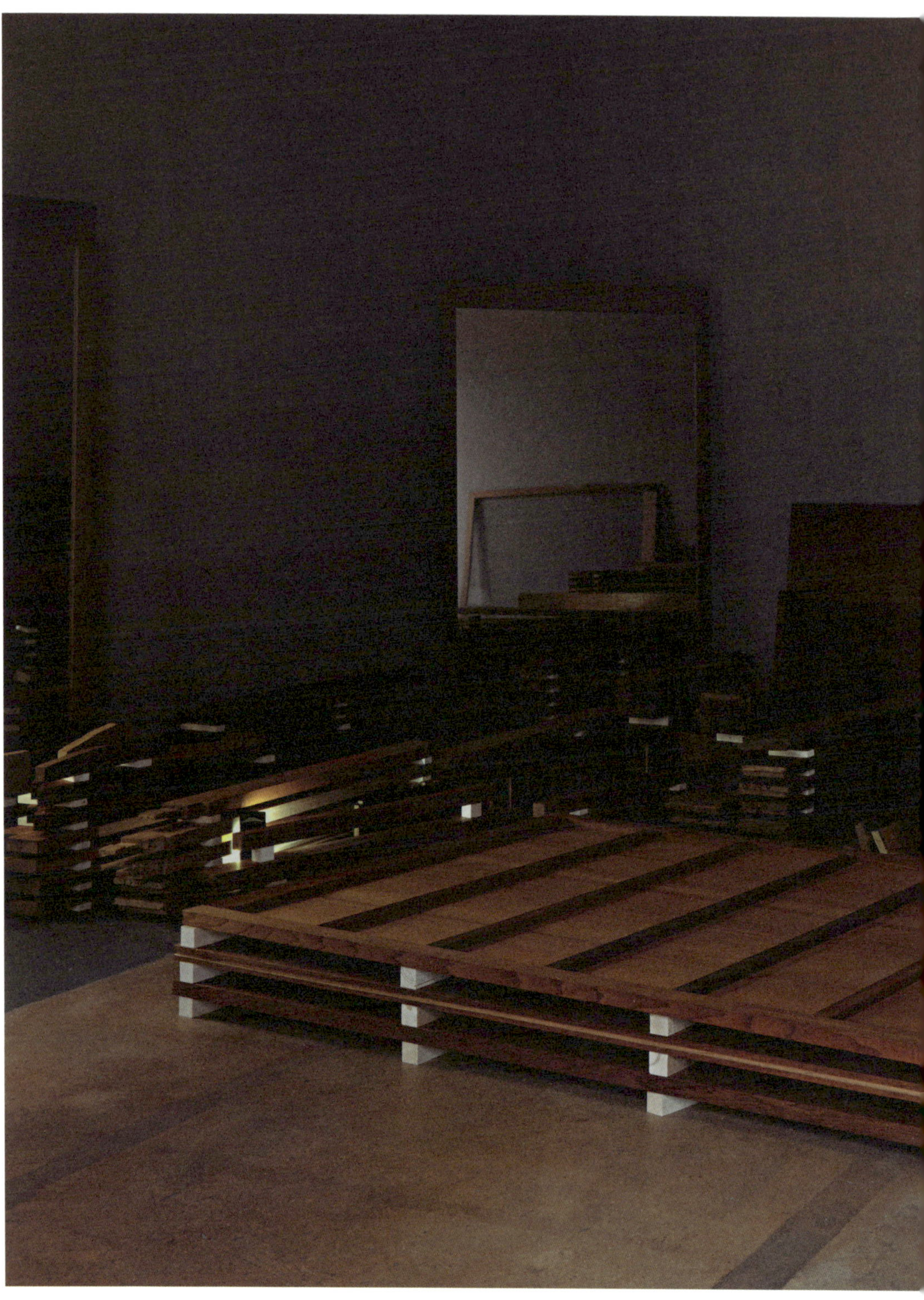

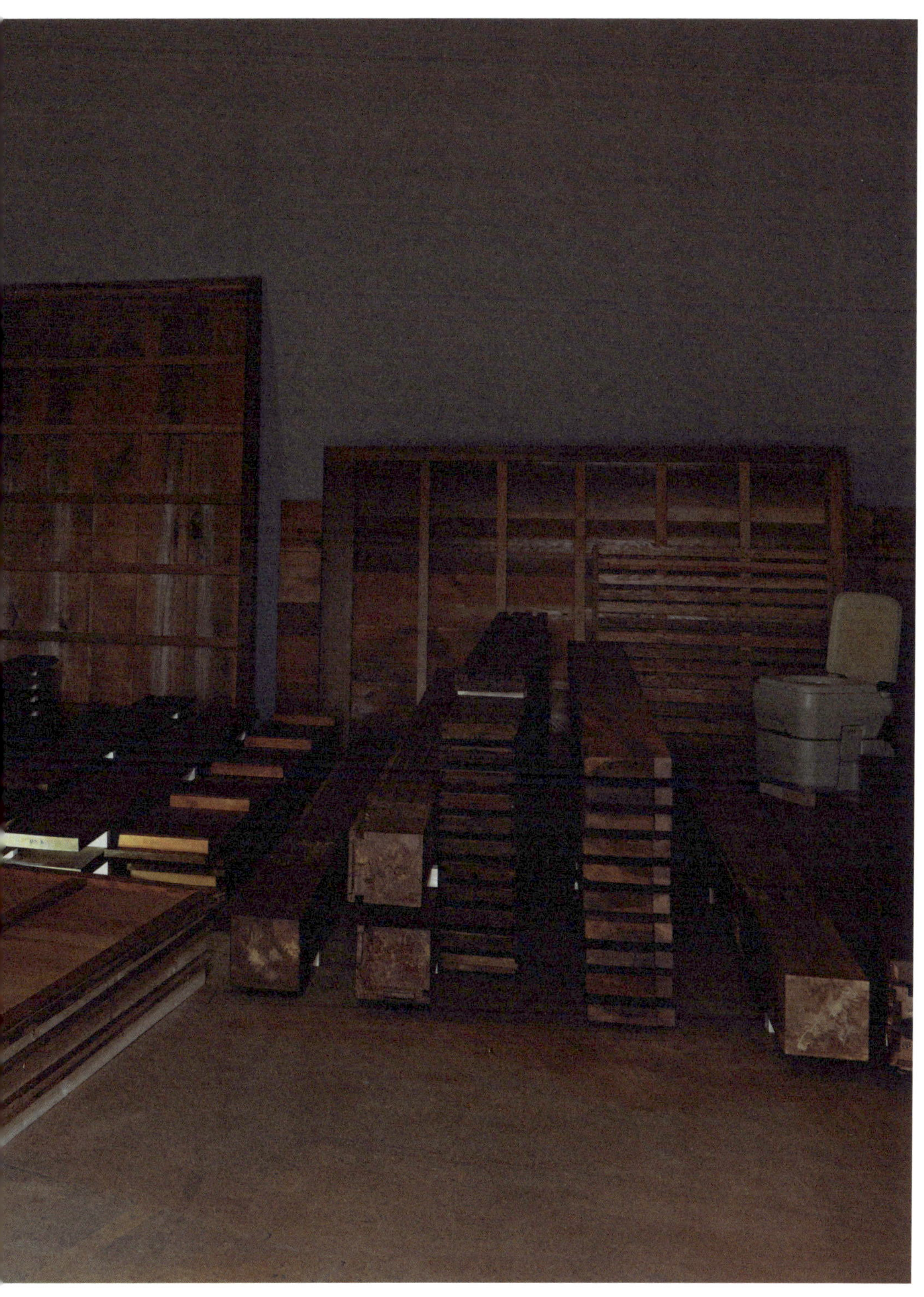

Maria Nordman, *Untitled, 1989-…*, 1989
coll. MAMCO, don Pierre Darier

MICHAEL C. MCMILLEN

In 1981, the Los Angeles County Museum of Art (LACMA) played host[1] to installations by artists including Michael Asher, Chris Burden, and Jonathan Borofsky. The exhibition also featured *Central Meridian* by Michael C. McMillen (b. 1946): an unlikely "garage" purporting to be a mid-20th-century American-style movie set, complete with a 1964 Dodge Dart with an electric fire crackling on the back seat. McMillen called the work a "cultural tomb"—a space long sealed off from the world and rediscovered by the visitor. LACMA presented this time capsule of an America so close and yet so far away as a subtle tribute to Edward Kienholz. The work, which went on display again at the same LA venue (not far from the home of the Californian Assemblage artists) in 2023, appears as if tormented by a quiet violence: "From the midst of his reified memories, McMillen successfully suggests an owner from the owned."[2]

The MAMCO collection includes two sculptures by McMillen: a wooden apartment door [ILL. P. 92] bearing the hand-painted inscription "Chamber of Revelation," and a trompe-l'œil submarine door [ILL. P. 93]. Both doors were originally part of *Entropic Taxi; The Final Destination*,[3] a large installation whose title evoked notions of science fiction. According to the inscriptions, the mysterious "Chamber of Revelations" was "the office of Dr. E.B. Monroe, Mt Ebo Observatory of Astronomic & Fortune." The wordplay spanned the intersection between reality and fiction, suggesting *The Island of Doctor Moreau* and the actress Marilyn Monroe. As with the installation at LACMA, the "taxi" was a diorama, an entire environment. As visitors passed through a door marked "Elsewhere," they left the white cube of the museum and entered a set, a completely different world. McMillen's approach here bore many similarities to that of his contemporary William Leavitt— one marked by their shared love for post-war America and a fascination with the centrality of cinema, and the illusions it produces, in Los Angeles. Unlike Leavitt, however, McMillen's work offers up a uniquely immersive and disorienting experience: "Artifice, violence, and nostalgia are the silent residents" of his installations.[4] His vision of the American Dream—represented by an assorted array of discarded and recycled objects, coupled with trompe-l'œil effects—reflects a critical viewpoint that is very much in keeping with the approach of the Assemblage artists that came before him.

—Julien Fronsacq

1   *The Museum as Site: Sixteen Projects,* curated by Stephanie Barron, Los Angeles County Museum of Art, 1981, p. 55.

2   Howard Singerman, "Art In Los Angeles," *Artforum,* March 1982.

3   Exhibited at the Palais de Tokyo, Paris, in 2014.

4   Susan C. Larsen, "Michael C. McMillen. Asherfaure Gallery," *Artforum,* February 1983.

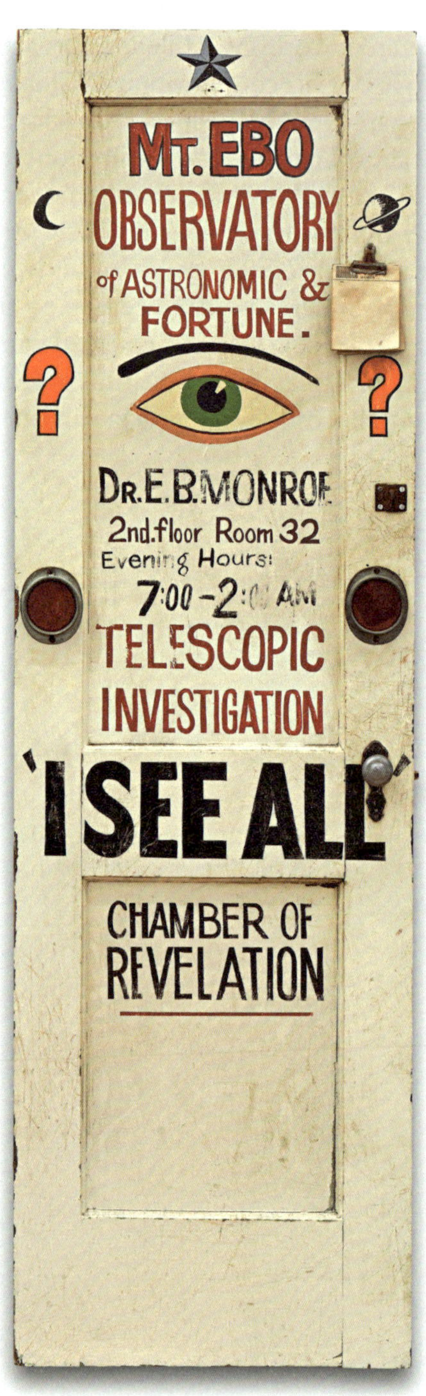

Michael McMillen, *Hand Lettered Door for Chamber of Revelation*, ca. 2001
coll. MAMCO, don Mary Ann et Hal Glicksman

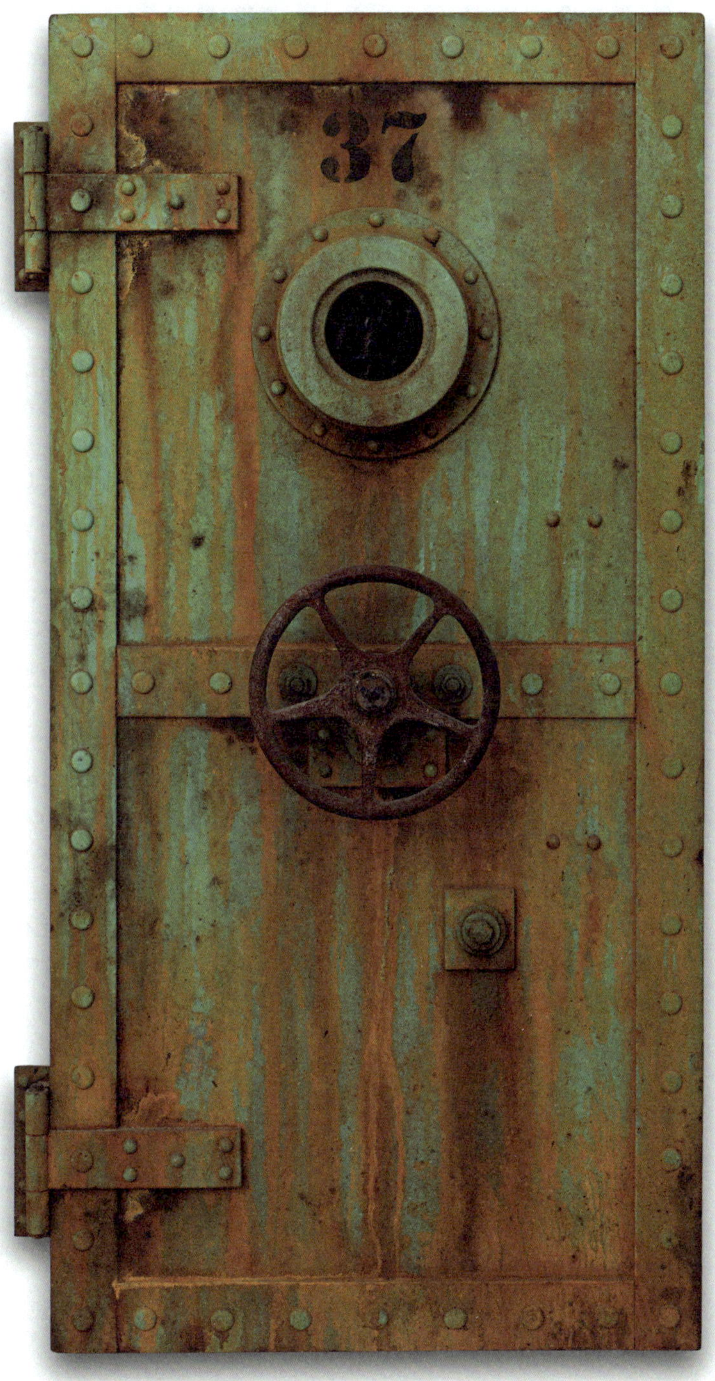

Michael McMillen, *Untitled*, ca. 2001
coll. MAMCO, don Mary Ann et Hal Glicksman

LIGHT AND SPACE

"Light and Space" is the name given to a loosely affiliated art movement that emerged in Los Angeles in the 1960s and 1970s, whose exponents were concerned with the relationship between art and the viewer's perception. The movement took its name from *Transparency, Reflection, Light, Space: Four Artists,* a 1971 group show at the UCLA University Art Gallery featuring Larry Bell, Robert Irwin, Craig Kauffman, and Peter Alexander. The works on display "served as liaison between the artists and the space they chose to animate."[1] More broadly, the movement bolstered and helped draw attention to the Southern California contemporary art scene, which had often been dismissed as lacking innovation until well into the post-war period.[2]

The majority of works associated with the movement were sculptures and installations, which offered the opportunity to fully engage viewers' bodies and senses under controlled conditions. These pieces promised immersive sensory and analytical experiences, making use of the available space and the properties of light, including its interplay with transparent and reflective surfaces. Members of the Light and Space group took advantage of post-war advances in aviation technology, showing a particular interest in the artistic possibilities offered by new materials such as resin, Plexiglas and neon lighting. Some of these works were so complex that they were developed with input from engineers.

Hal Glicksman witnessed the emergence of Light and Space during his time as a curator, organizing boundary-pushing exhibitions that earned him recognition as a leading figure in the

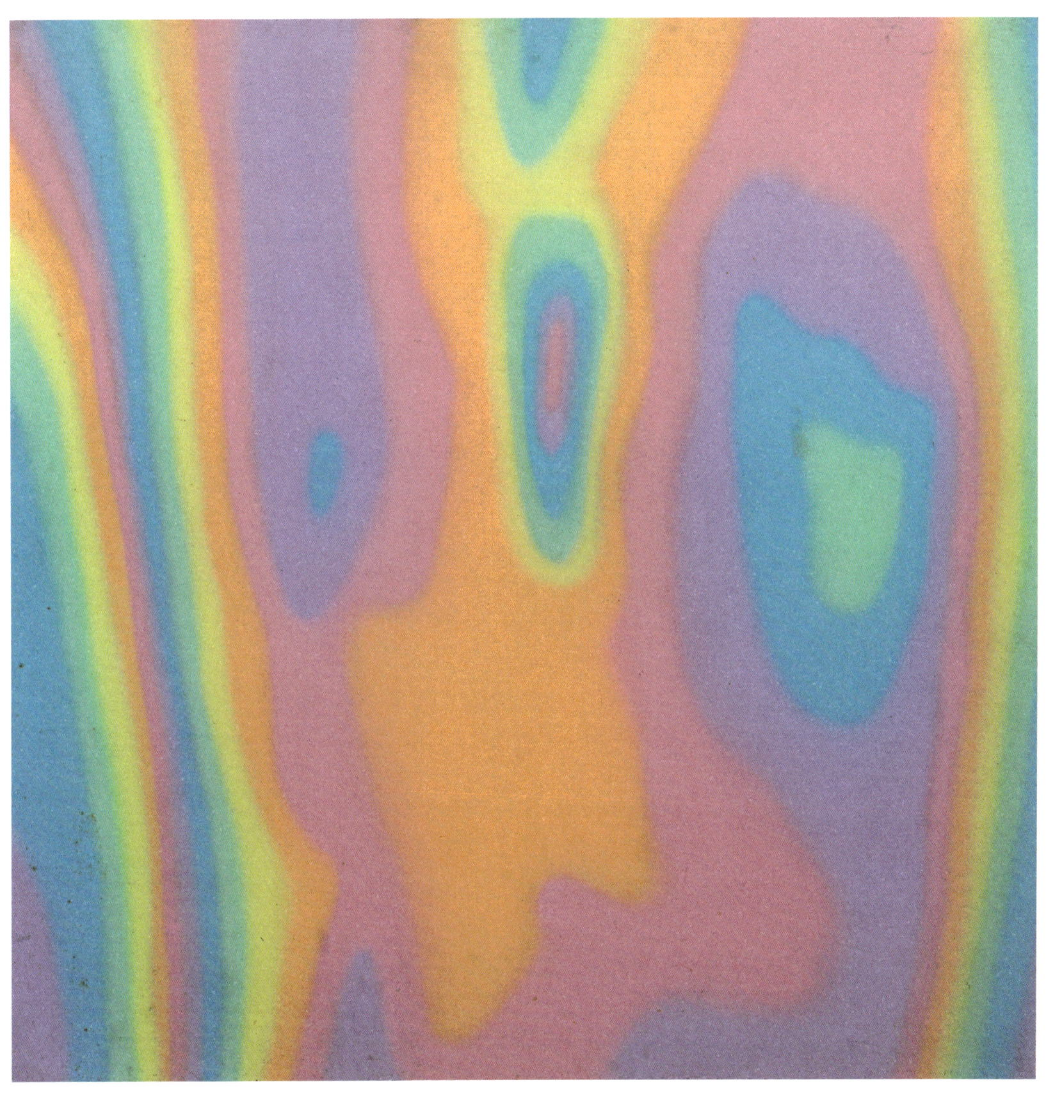

Tom Eatherton, *Untitled*, n.d.
coll. MAMCO, don Mary Ann et Hal Glicksman

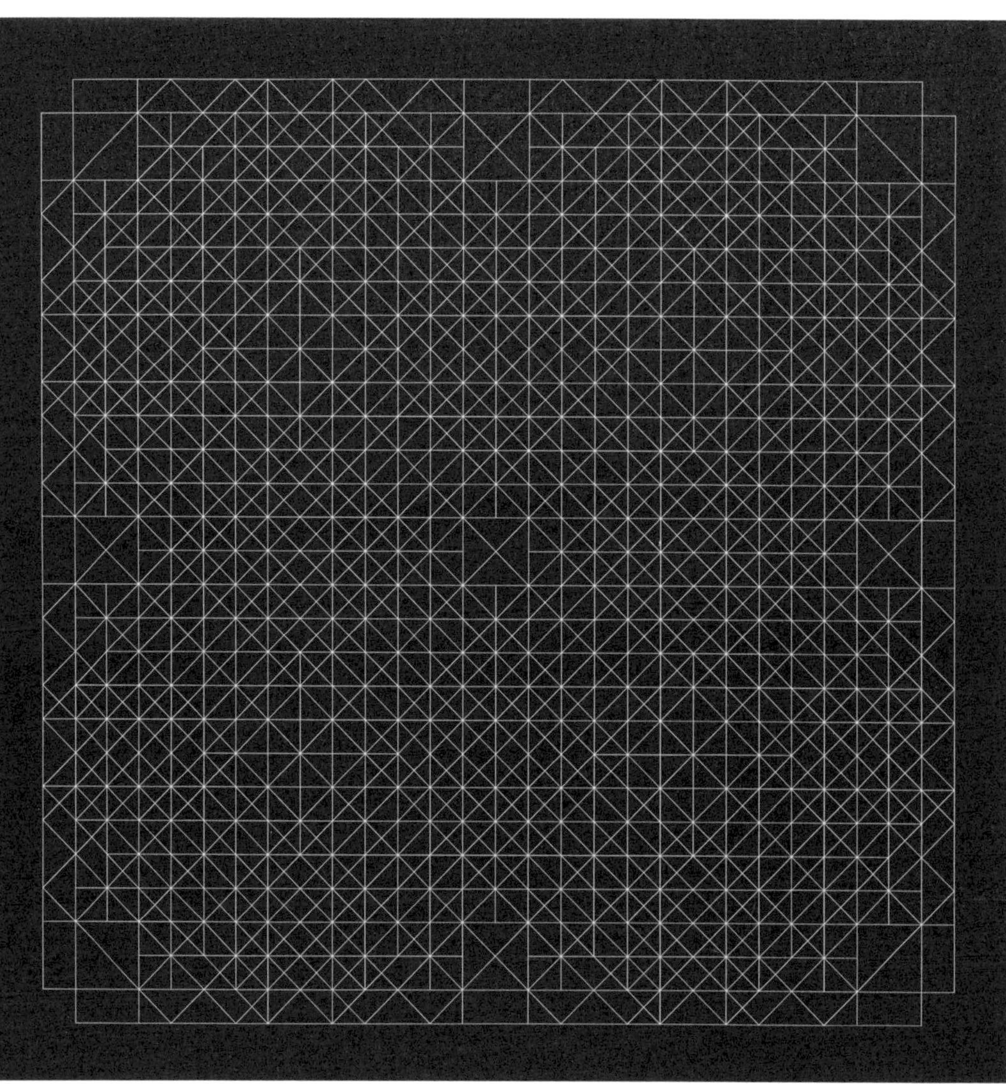

Tom Eatherton, *Untitled*, n.d.
coll. MAMCO, don Mary Ann et Hal Glicksman

movement's rise to prominence. Starting in the late 1960s, he curated shows featuring names such as Judy Chicago, Ron Cooper, Peter Alexander, Robert Irwin, Tom Eatherton, Larry Bell, and Eric Orr.[3]

The donation from the Glicksman collection includes several pieces that testify to this relationship, including works on paper by Larry Bell [ILL. P. 101], Tom Eatherton [ILL. P. 95–96], and Patrick Hogan, as well as a series of three hand-finished lithographs produced by Peter Alexander for his *Sunsets* exhibition at the UC Irvine Art Gallery in 1974. Also part of the donation are a number of archive documents, including a poster created by Eric Orr for his 1984 show at the University Art Gallery, San Diego State University (*Eric Orr: A Twenty-year Survey*), and a limited-edition print of a technical drawing of Newton Harrison's installation for the 1971 *Art & Technology* exhibition at the Los Angeles County Museum of Art that Glicksman co-curated.

— Laura Weber

1   *Transparency, Reflection, Light, Space: Four Artists*, Los Angeles: UCLA Art Galleries, 1971.

2   Peter Plagens, *Sunshine Muse: Contemporary Art of the West Coast*, New York: Praeger Publishers, 1974, p. 117.

3   Glicksman curated shows for the following Light and Space artists (listed in chronological order): Judy Chicago (1969, Pomona College Art Gallery), Ron Cooper (1969, Pomona College Art Gallery), Peter Alexander (1974, UC Irvine Art Gallery), Tom Eatherton (1970, Pomona College Art Gallery; 1975, UC Irvine Art Gallery; 1981, Percept), Robert Irwin (1970, Pomona College Art Gallery), Larry Bell (1973, UC Irvine Art Gallery), and Eric Orr (1987, UC Irvine Art Gallery).

TOM EATHERTON

Tom Eatherton (1934–2023) was a lesser-known figure of the Light and Space movement. It was as an art student at UCLA that he met Hal Glicksman in the late 1950s, and the two remained close throughout the artist's life. After graduating, Eatherton began producing Abstract Expressionist paintings before quickly switching his focus to light installation art. As he explained it, immersion and experience came to occupy a central place in his practice: "I don't want to look at [paintings] from the outside. I want to look at them from the inside. [...] I work with people's perceptions in order to create an experience."[1]

Eatherton produced three immersive installations commissioned by Glicksman. But it was his exhibit for his first show, *Rise,* held in 1970 at the Pomona College Art Gallery, that would ultimately be remembered as one of the most important works of his career.[2] It consisted of an oval-shaped room with two large, curved panels made from two layers of nylon diffusion material that filtered light from incandescent bulbs behind them, creating a meditative atmosphere bathed in soft, bluish tones, and producing an effect akin to an optical illusion. Art critic Melinda Wortz described this "perceptual surprise" in the following terms: "Not only do these white curved walls appear to be glowing with light in the otherwise darkened room, but they also appear to be breathing—up and down."[3]

Three untitled drawings, produced using pastel or gouache between 1985 and 1993, were donated from the Glicksman collection to the Kunsthaus Pasquart in Biel/Bienne [ILL. P. 10–11]. These drawings feature a moiré pattern in the colors of the rainbow, evoking the dispersion of light. MAMCO received a similar work, albeit larger in size and executed in acrylic spray paint [ILL. P. 95]. The donation also includes a digital print of the artist's *Diamond Series* (1993–1999) [ILL. P. 96], a minimalist, complex, computer-generated composition of squares that placed Eatherton at the forefront of the then-emerging field of digital art.

— Laura Weber

1   "Tom Eatherton interviewed by David Pagel," *It Happened at Pomona: Art at the Edge of Los Angeles, 1969–1973*, Claremont: Pomona College Museum of Art, p. 146–149.

2   The other two installations were *Guide* (UC Irvine Art Gallery, 1974), and a piece for a 1981 solo show at Percept, an independent exhibition space directed by Glicksman in 1981 and 1982. The curator also wanted to show *Rise* again in the same exhibition.

3   Melinda Wortz, *Art News*, Vol. 81, No. 3, 1982.

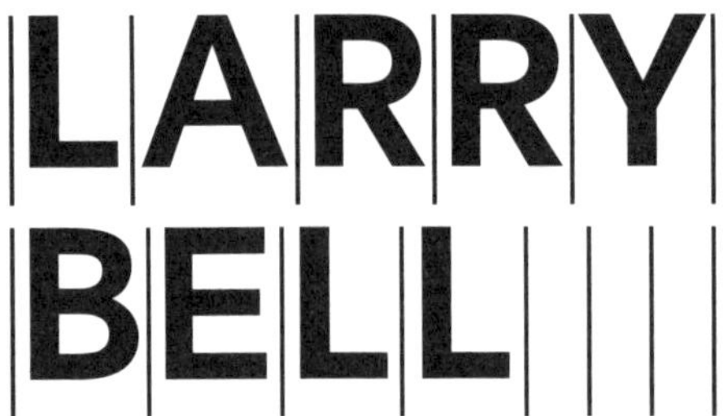

LARRY BELL

Larry Bell (b. 1939) became a leading figure in the California art world and, to quote the critic Peter Plagens, "the embodiment of the L.A. Look."[1] In the late 1950s, he studied at the Chouinard Art Institute under Robert Irwin, whose theories on perception made a lasting impression on the young artist. Bell held his first solo show in 1962 at the Ferus Gallery, a leading venue of the Los Angeles avant-garde scene. The attention he drew paved the way to an exhibition at New York's Pace Gallery five years later. In 1974, Bell was invited by Hal Glicksman—the director of the UC Irvine Art Gallery at the time—to contribute to a sound installation intended to alter visitors' spatial perception. The donation from the Glicksman collection includes a poster from this collaborative project: a floor plan of the gallery, over which the artist has sketched a self-portrait and added his signature.

The properties of light and its interactions with surfaces remained a central theme of Bell's work. After producing a series of experimental shaped canvases, he turned to sculpture, preferring to work with glass on account of its ability to simultaneously reflect, absorb, and transmit light, and, above all, to change in appearance depending on its environment and the angle from which it is viewed. Bell also employed a vacuum-coating technique developed for the aviation industry to apply a thin metal film onto the surface of the glass, which altered how the color spectrum was reflected.

The donation also includes several later works on paper, from a period of Bell's career in which he abandoned sculpture and

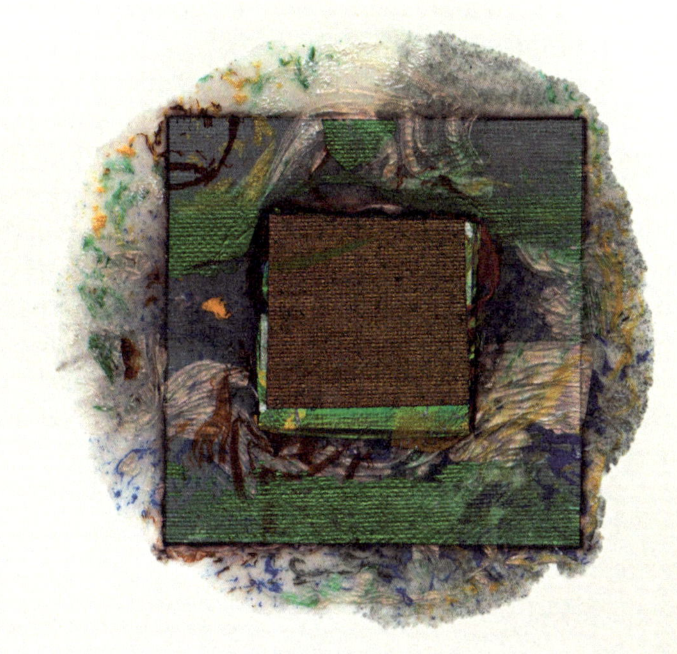

Larry Bell, *Untitled*, 1998
coll. MAMCO, don Mary Ann et Hal Glicksman

returned to working in two-dimensional formats. These collages, which are part of the artist's *Fractions* series (1996–2000, ILL. P. 101), were made from recycled fragments of older pieces. Bell assembled them on a paper background and then covered it all with several layers of transparent acrylic film. These playful experiments gave rise to more than 10,000 "random, spontaneous and improvised" images.[2]

Also among the donated works is a collection of photographs—another of Bell's favorite media. His book *Animated Discourse* (1975), produced in conjunction with Guy de Cointet, features a series of panoramas taken in Bell's Venice studio in 1968, with the human subjects striking overacted poses of the kind typically seen in soap operas. These long, slim strips are divided into sections, each containing a separate photo. In that sense, they function like a cryptic storyboard devised by de Cointet, with Bell taking the photographs and applying the silver coating. These panoramas touch on themes involving peripheral vision—a concept Bell first explored in his earlier sculptures.

— Laura Weber

1   "But it was Larry Bell who stood, in the mid-sixties, as the embodiment of the L.A. Look, both in its initial phase and as it developed," Peter Plagens, *Sunshine Muse: Contemporary Art of the West Coast,* New York: Praeger Publishers, 1974, p. 125–126.

2   Larry Bell, "Des mois de réflexions," in *Larry Bell,* Nîmes: Carré d'Art – Musée d'art contemporain de Nîmes, 2011, p. 11.

Larry Bell

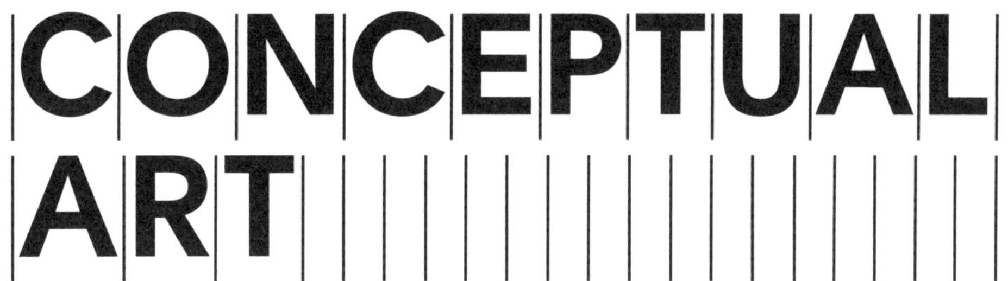

GUY DE COINTET

French artist Guy de Cointet (1934–1983) served as an assistant to sculptor Larry Bell. In 1965, he followed Bell to Los Angeles, where he lived for the rest of his life. He developed an early interest in cryptology and typography, which he used as tools for transforming words into images and for giving form to color. He produced large drawings of cryptic writings whose titles appeared to offer the key to deciphering them. De Cointet's interest in devising codes led him to develop these drawings into entire books of "typoetry." Although they contained no form of comprehensible language that might prompt anyone to read them, it was nevertheless on these works that he would base his performances.

The first took place in Paris, in 1973: as an actress played with a set of silkscreen-printed red letters affixed to the wall, "CIZEGHOH TUR NDJMB," she struck poses typical of those found in fashion magazines. In the same year, this time exploring the linguistic aspect of his work, de Cointet cast a dwarf actor as the author of *ESPAHOR LEDET KO ULUNER*. The inspiration for his writings and plays came from real life—from advertising and soap operas, to which he applied the cut-up technique in the style of William Burroughs and Brion Gysin.

De Cointet's work was the catalyst that brought Hal Glicksman and Mary Ann Duganne together. In 1976, the self-taught actress performed two of his plays: *At Sunrise a Cry Was Heard* and *Ethiopia*. In the space of six years, she took part in seven of de Cointet's productions. The mock-up used to advertise the last of these—*Five Sisters*—is held in MAMCO's collection. The museum

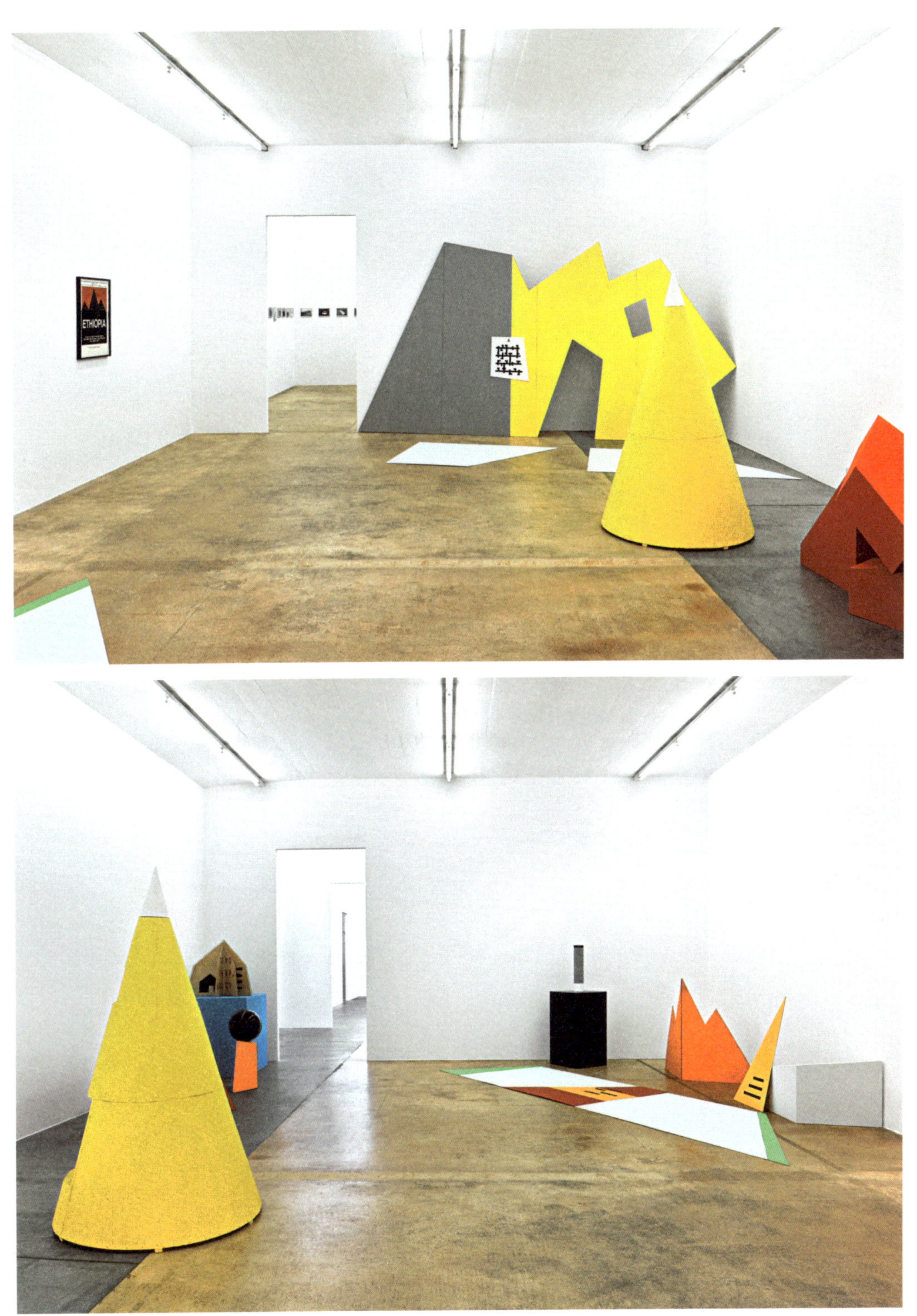

Guy de Cointet, Robert Wilhite, *Ethiopia*, 1976-2004
coll. MAMCO

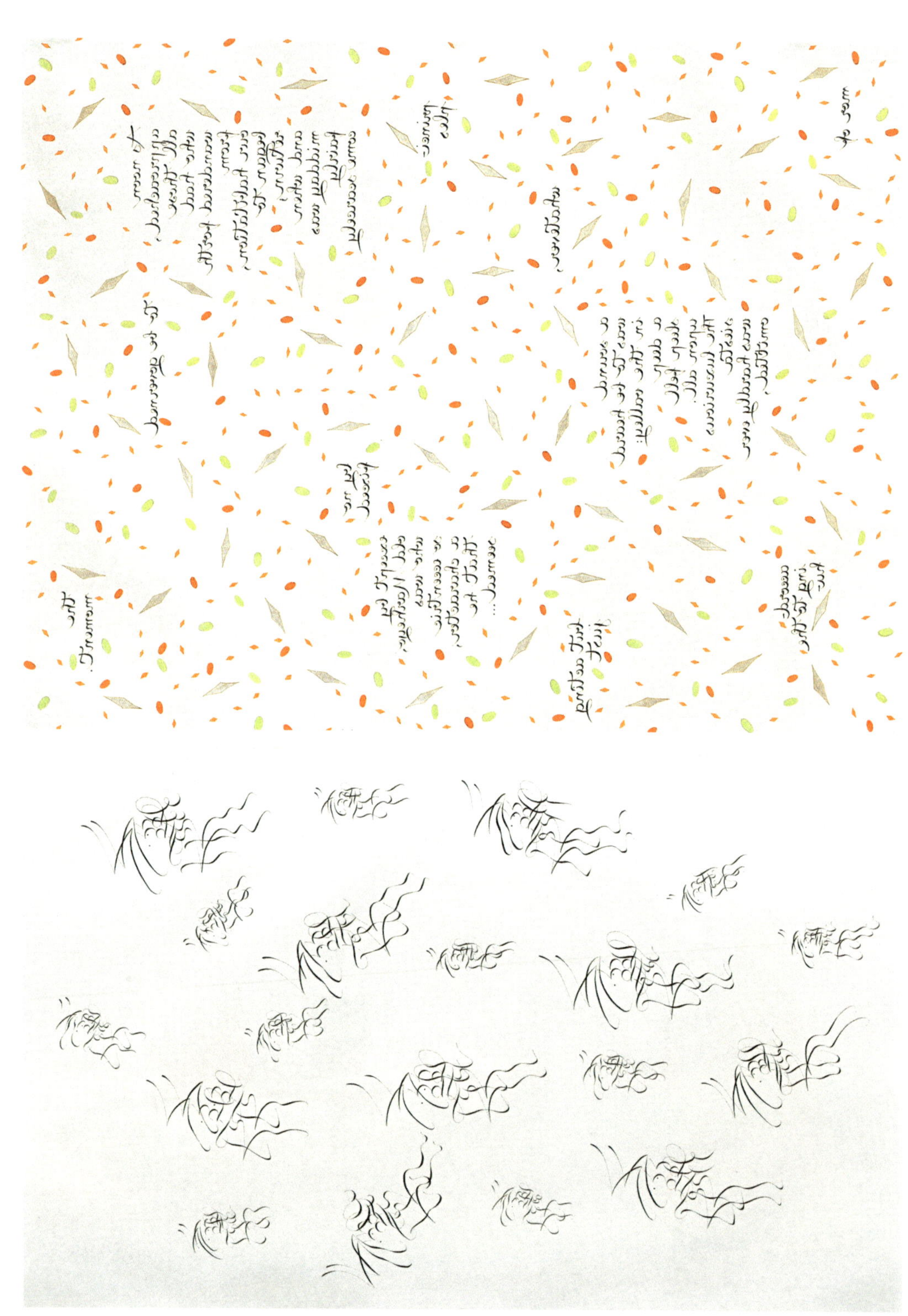

Guy de Cointet, *A deep sleep fall upon all…*, 1982
coll. MAMCO, don Mary Ann et Hal Glicksman
Guy de Cointet, *Night*, ca. 1982
coll. MAMCO, don Mary Ann et Hal Glicksman

already possessed a significant number of the artist's works, including paintings, drawings, and the set for *Ethiopia*. This corpus has been expanded thanks to the donations from the Glicksman collection, which comprise the prototype book for *Ethiopia*, various ephemera, and four drawings from the 1980s.

Staged for the first time in Los Angeles in 1976, *Ethiopia* was the first of Guy de Cointet's performance pieces to consist of several acts and to use a number of actors. It was also the first of several collaborations with Robert Wilhite, who handled the musical side of the works. On stage, the objects that made up the set replaced books as elements on which the storyline turned. Their status quickly became ambiguous: while the actors used and commented on them, they retained a degree of autonomy. In these plays with no real plot in the traditional sense, it was the interactions—or the symbiosis, even—between the objects themselves and with the actors that constituted the core of the work. A blonde woman, a Latin-American man, and an African-American man, chosen to represent archetypal figures, recounted family stories. They brought the objects to life during the performance. But, once this was over, these same objects became sculptures, retaining only their spatial relationships as a recollection of the performance—those very same relationships that served to trigger situations.

— Sophie Costes

INSTITUTIONAL CRITIQUE

Institutional critique is a practice associated with the Conceptual art of the 1970s, by which the focus shifts away from aesthetic considerations related to works of art and toward the physical and ideological influences of the exhibition space. Artists involved in this approach critically inquire into the setting in which art is displayed—be it the architecture of the museum or gallery, or the economic system in which the venue operates. The term first appeared in the 1980s in reference to a generation of U.S. artists such as Andrea Fraser, Louise Lawler, Renée Green, and Fred Wilson, all of whom were associated with the Whitney Museum of American Art's Independent Study Program. This group claimed to carry the legacy of an earlier generation of artists that emerged on both sides of the Atlantic in the late 1960s and included names like Marcel Broodthaers, Daniel Buren, Hans Haacke, and Michael Asher.

Hal Glicksman collaborated with members of this earlier generation. In February 1970, he exhibited works by Michael Asher at the Pomona College Art Gallery, in what was the artist's first major museum or gallery show. Later, as the director of the Otis Art Institute, Glicksman curated exhibitions in which he encouraged other artists to treat the gallery as a medium in its own right. In 1975, for instance, the venue hosted two installations by Dan Graham—*Present Continuous Past(s)* and *Yesterday/Today*—that used mirrors and cameras to challenge the relationship between viewer and subject. The accompanying publication, entitled *For Publication,* reproduced a series of Graham's projects from the

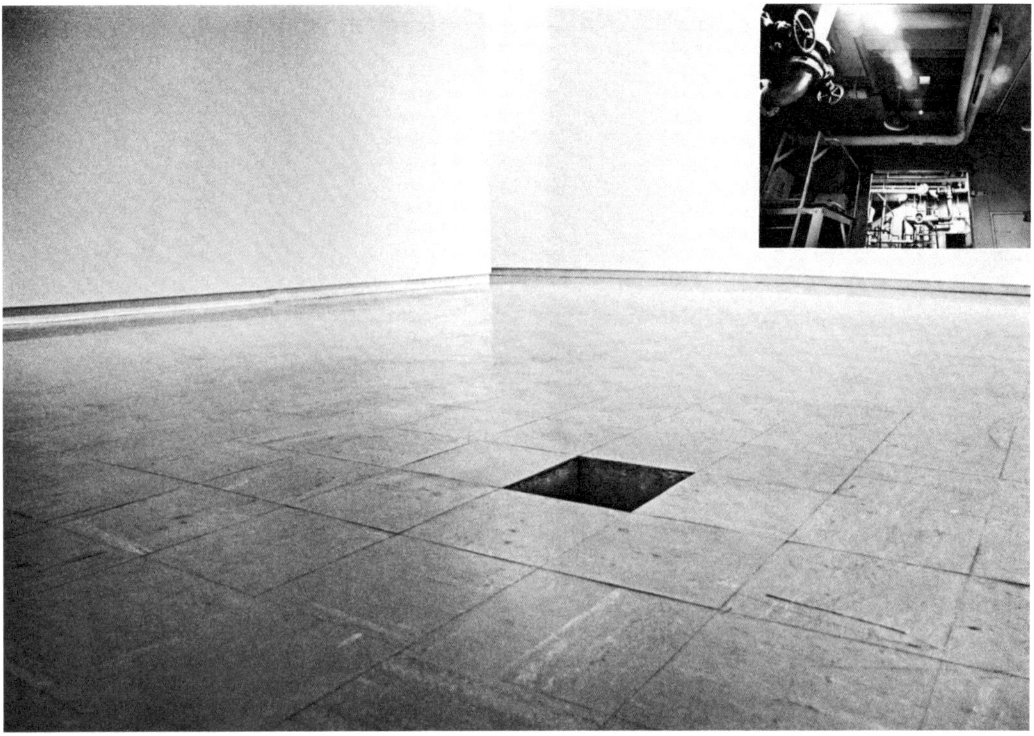

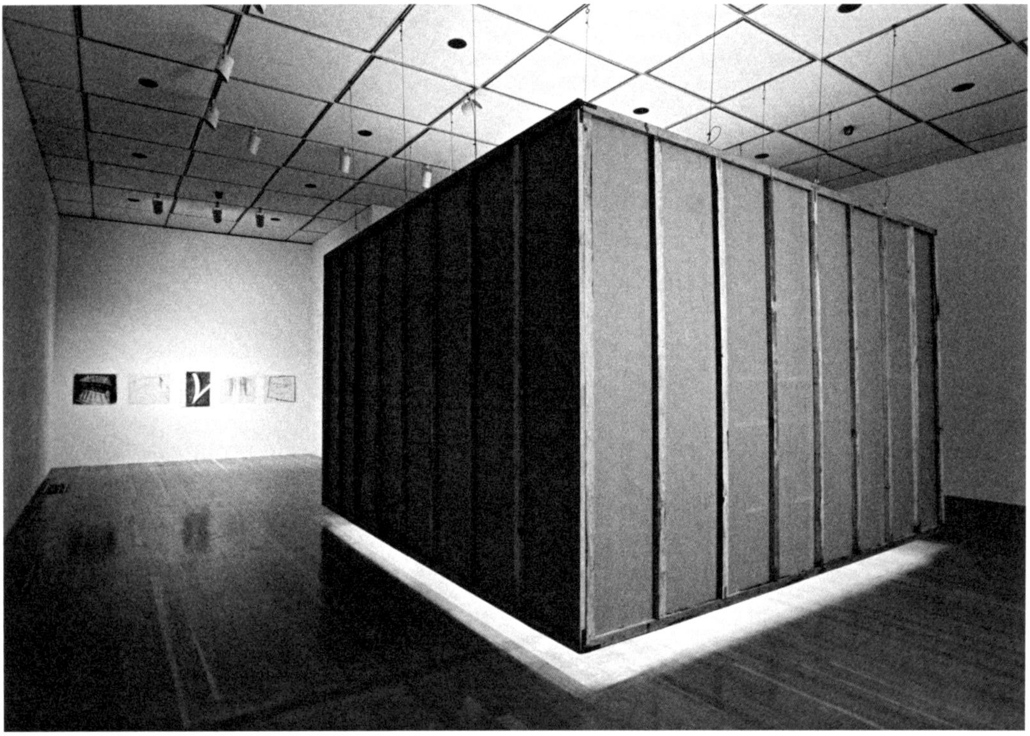

Jane Reynolds, installation view, Otis Art Institute, 1976
Don Hal Glicksman. Getty Research Institute, Los Angeles (2009.M.5)
Bruce Nauman, *Floating Room*, University of California, Irvine, 1973
Don Hal Glicksman. Getty Research Institute, Los Angeles (2009.M.5)

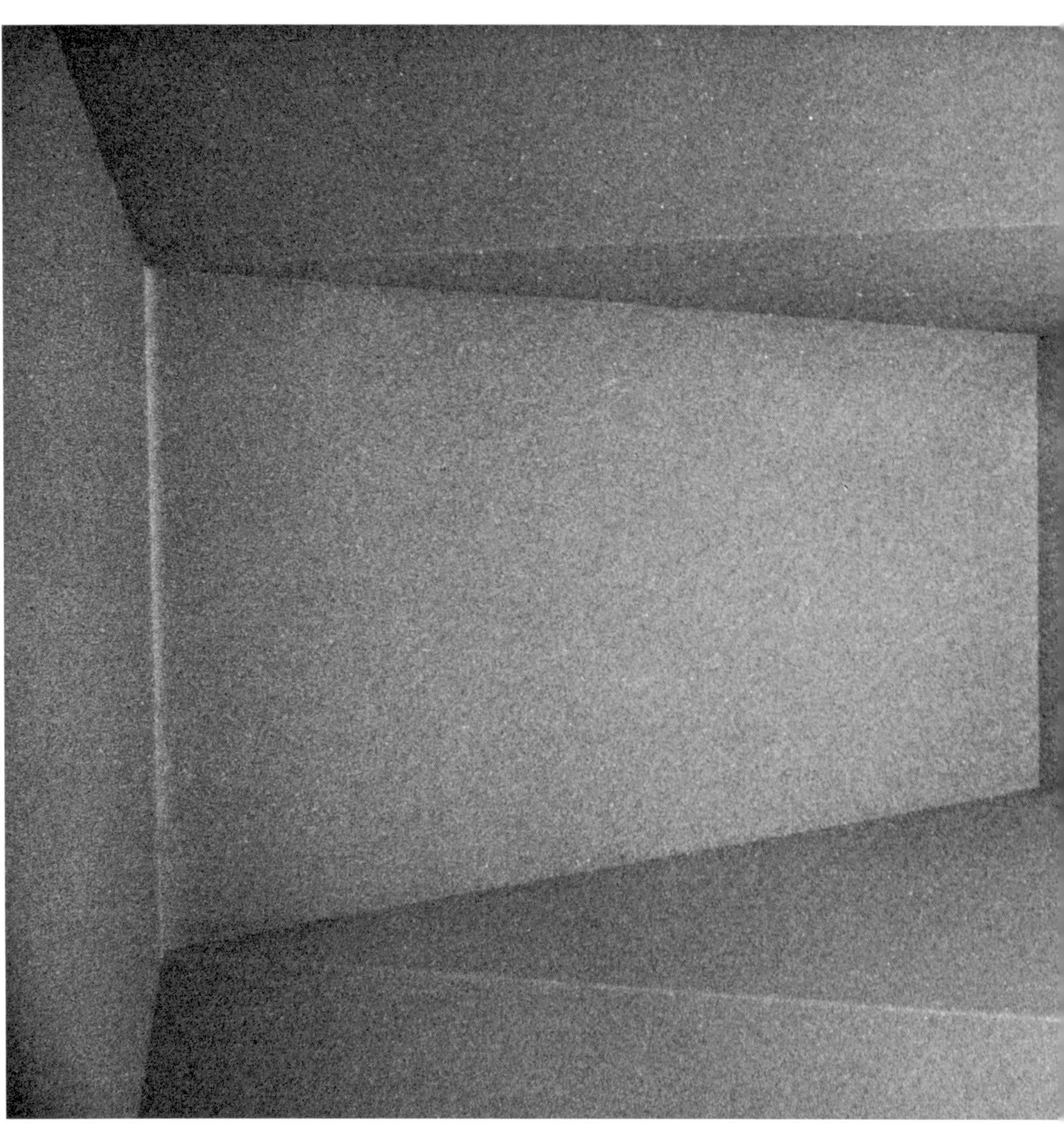

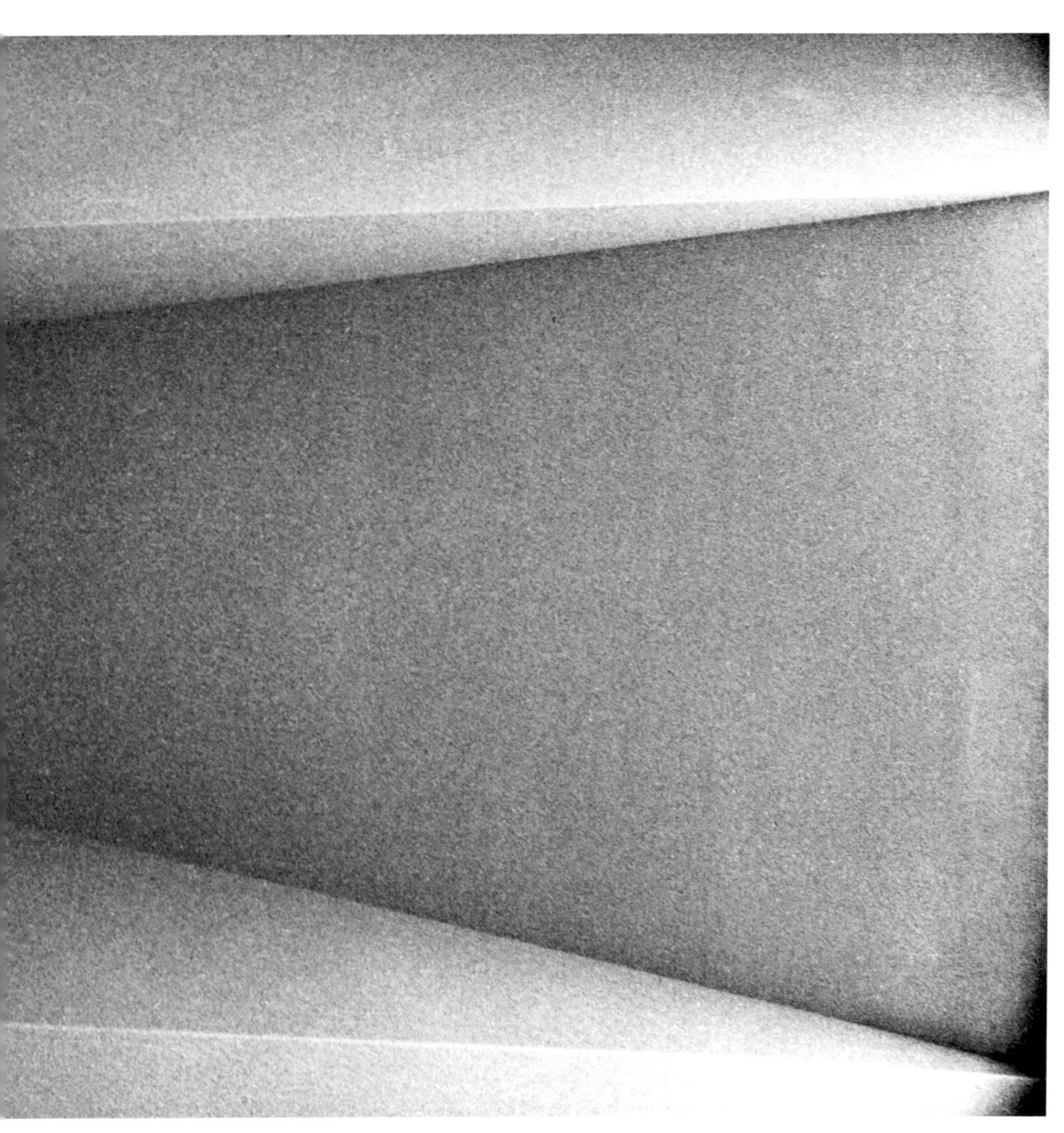

Maria Nordman, *Saddleback Mountain*, University of California, Irvine, 1973
Don Hal Glicksman. Getty Research Institute, Los Angeles (2009.M.5)

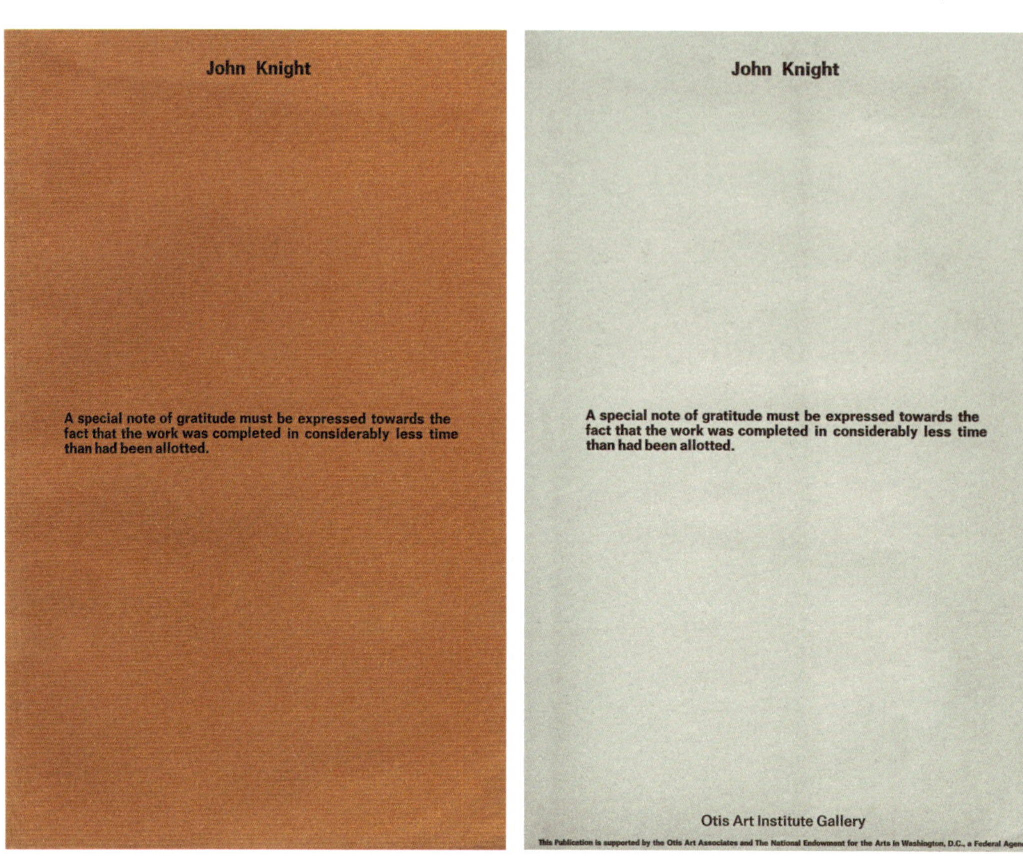

John Knight, *A special note of gratitude must be expressed towards the fact that the work was completed in considerably less time than had been allotted,* Otis Art Institute, 1977
coll. MAMCO, don Mary Ann et Hal Glicksman

1960s that used materials from print media. For her 1976 show at the same venue, Jane Reynolds opened up a 23 x 23 cm hole in the floor of the otherwise empty exhibition space. The aperture was deep enough to reveal the sights and sounds of the college's vast underfloor furnace. The move almost cost Glicksman his job. In 1977, the venue hosted *Frost and Defrost,* an installation by Daniel Buren. The artist removed the ceiling tiles from the gallery and backed them with striped paper. The tiles were then methodically returned to their place in the ceiling over the course of 35 days. By the end of the exhibition, the space appeared completely empty. In 1978, John Knight exhibited the Otis Art Institute's mailing list, presenting it exactly as it was actually printed: not simply in alphabetical order, but in a sequence of membership categories. The work took the form of a book in which Knight listed all the names preceding his own. Under each name, he indicated a particular time and day, effectively dividing the exhibition temporally between different individuals. The book was placed in the window display at the entrance to the venue for the duration of the show [ILL. P. 114].

These conceptual, site-specific works were by nature immaterial. The Glicksman collection nevertheless contains publications, postcards, plans, and sketches that testify to their existence, including some items signed and dedicated by the artists.

— Paul Bernard

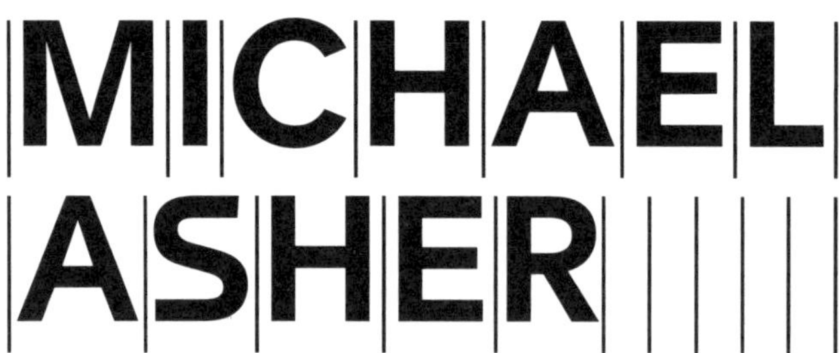

MICHAEL ASHER

Michael Asher (1943–2012) began his career during the Post-Minimalist period of the late 1960s. The relationship between his works and the context in which they were shown was a constant feature of his radical practice. Asher would offer up a revelation by drawing attention to an absent, intangible or missing feature of a particular space, "in the hope of increasing his viewers' perception of that environment's context, and perhaps also deepening their understanding of the conventions and structures that make contemporary art visible and meaningful." While his approach bore some of the hallmarks of Minimalism, his aim was to draw the viewer's gaze not to a specific object but to the environment itself. Each of Asher's works—part in-situ installation, part institutional critique—cast a critical eye on a social or political theme.

Asher's installation for his 1970 show at Pomona College Art Gallery was a stand-out example of site-specific critique. The artist reconfigured the gallery by adding walls and removing its doors, bringing noise, sunlight, and air into the space, and leaving it accessible around the clock. The venue was transformed into two triangular spaces joined at their apexes by a narrow opening, which visitors had to pass through to move from one section to the other. Asher conceived this setup as a critique both of the gatekeeping role played by conventional galleries and museums, and of the mass-production and commodification of art.

The Glicksman collection includes a series of cyanotype blueprints of Asher's technical drawings [ILL. P. 117]. One of them,

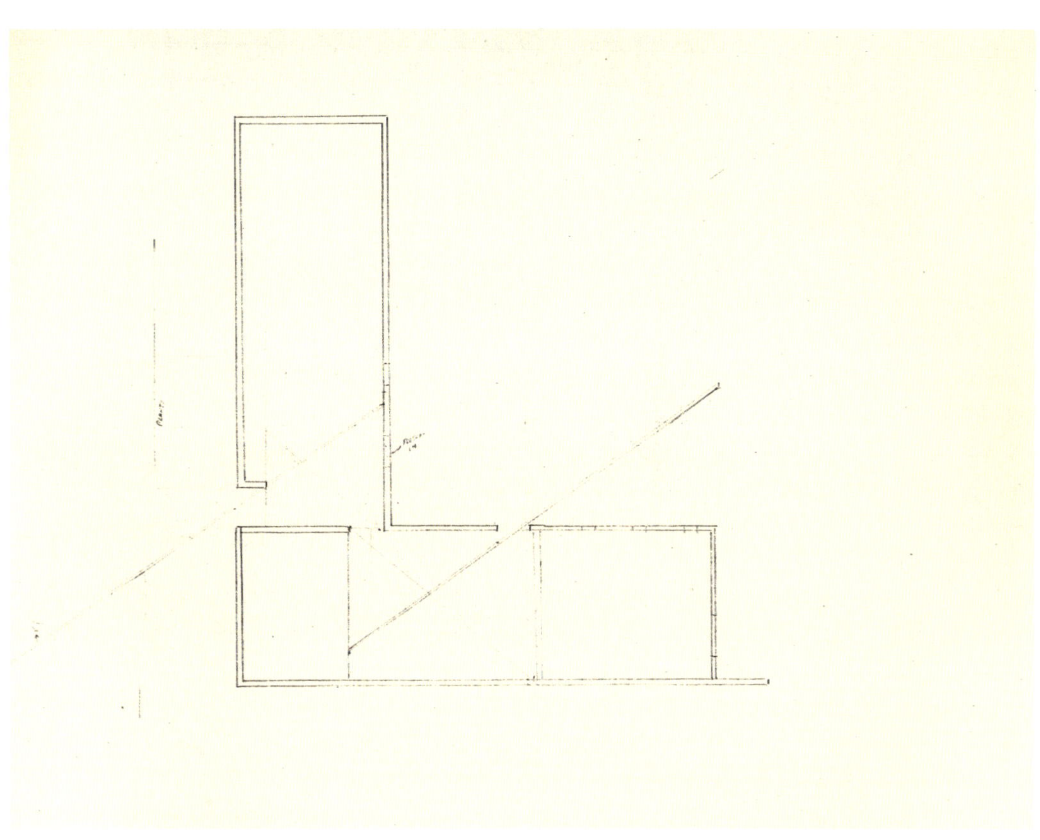

Michael Asher, *Final Work for Pomona College Museum of Art*, 1970
Fondation Collection Centre PasquArt

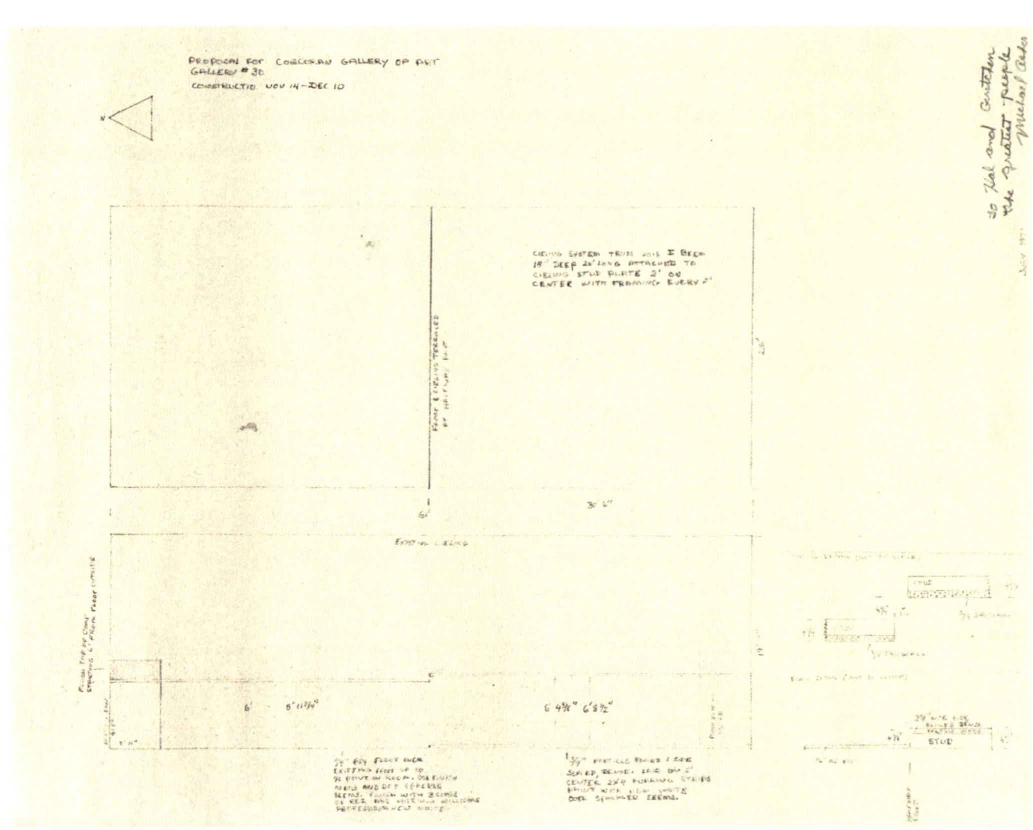

Michael Asher, *Unrealized Proposals for Corcoran Gallery of Art*, 1969
coll. MAMCO, don Mary Ann et Hal Glicksman

signed by the artist, depicts an installation at the Pomona College Art Gallery, although the layout differs from the end product exhibited in 1970. Other blueprints relate to unfinished projects for the Corcoran Gallery of Art in Washington, D.C., where Glicksman served briefly as associate director between 1970 and 1972 [ILL. P. 118].

— Jenna Paratte

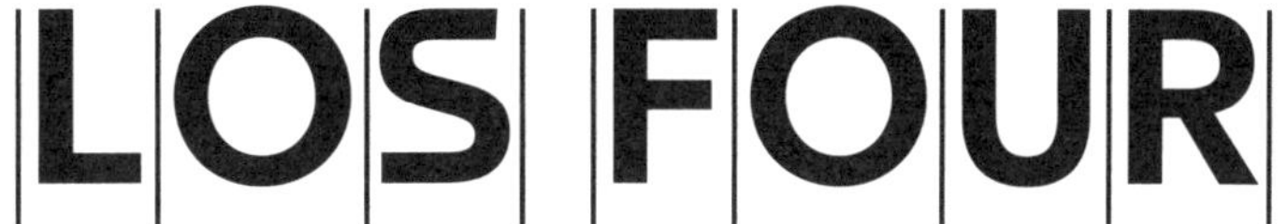

Gala Mayí-Miranda, Paul Bernard

Los Four was an artist collective founded in 1972 by Gilbert "Magú" Luján (1940–2011), Carlos Almaraz (1941–1989), Frank Romero (b. 1941), and Roberto "Beto" de la Rocha (b. 1937). The four members shared a background in graffiti art. They became the first group to claim a Chicano identity. At the time, Luján was studying under Hal Glicksman at UC Irvine. He persuaded the curator to host the collective's first show there in 1973. An expanded version of the exhibition was held at the Los Angeles County Museum of Art (LACMA) in 1974. The catalog for both shows took the form of a vast *leporello*, a folded and pleated paper book. It contained photographs from the artists' day-to-day lives as well as their biographies, written in mixed Spanish-and-English sentences. The four artists identified with *barrio* (ghetto) culture and emphasized their art-school backgrounds. Only Almaraz mentioned having been born in Mexico, noting that he had spent just six months there.

The Los Four logo, spraypainted and used on the poster for the 1973 and 1974 shows, was a joint effort by all four members: de la Rocha devised the initial design, Romero and Luján executed it on a wall and on paper, and Almaraz added a few finishing touches. This collaborative approach, which was common in the world of Street art, also signaled an attempt by the collective to distance themselves from artistic individualism and to seek out a shared culture characterized by symbols and a specific imagined reality. The group was instrumental in bringing Chicano culture into the mainstream U.S. art world. Judithe Hernández (b. 1948) joined the group following the show at LACMA, making Los Four one of only two major Chicano artist collectives to have a female member.[1] The donation from the Glicksman collection includes several works dealing with the artists' cultural heritage, the exploitation of agricultural laborers, and Mexican folklore.

Returning to Aztlán [ILL. P. 124-125] is a 200-copy silkscreen print signed "Magú" and dated 1983. The work is a brightly colored map of the lands from which the Nahuatl-speaking peoples, including the Mexica, migrated toward the Central Valleys and nearby valleys of present-day Mexico prior to the 16th century.

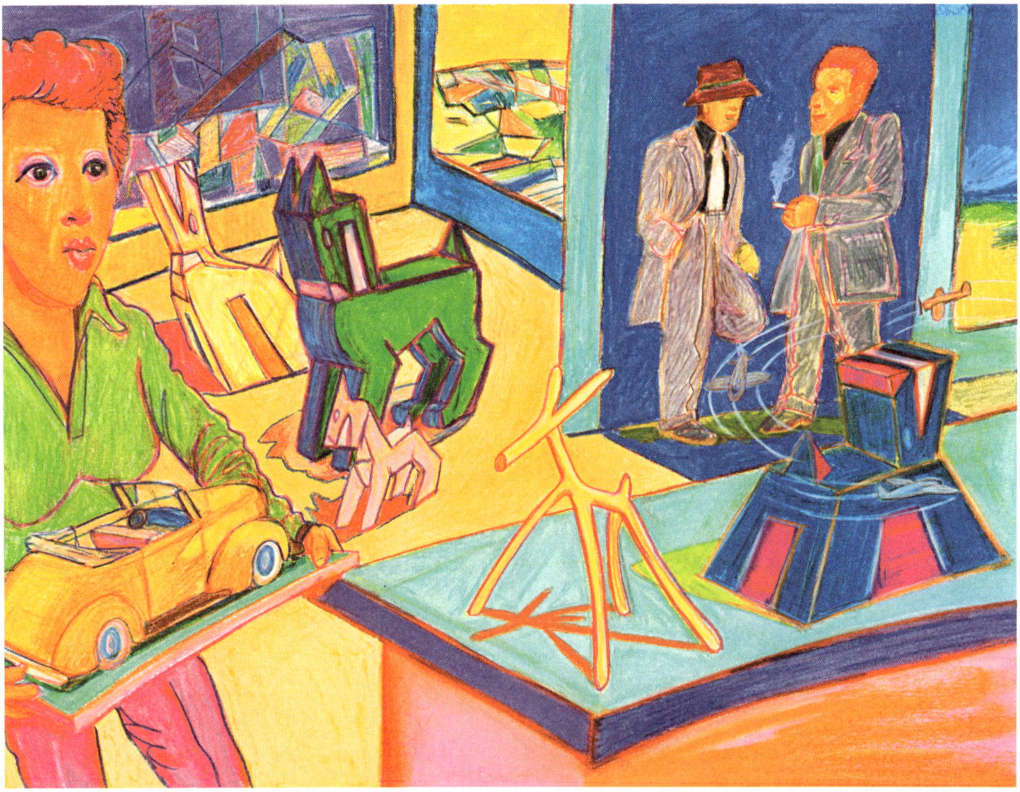

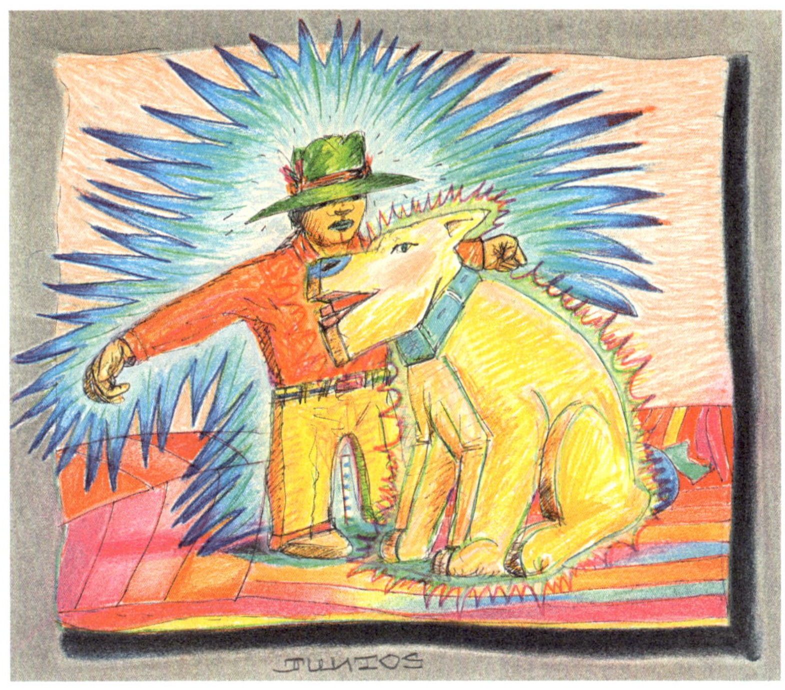

Gilbert "Magu" Luján, *Untitled*, 1982
Gilbert "Magu" Luján, *Juntos*, 1985
Fondation Collection Centre PasquArt

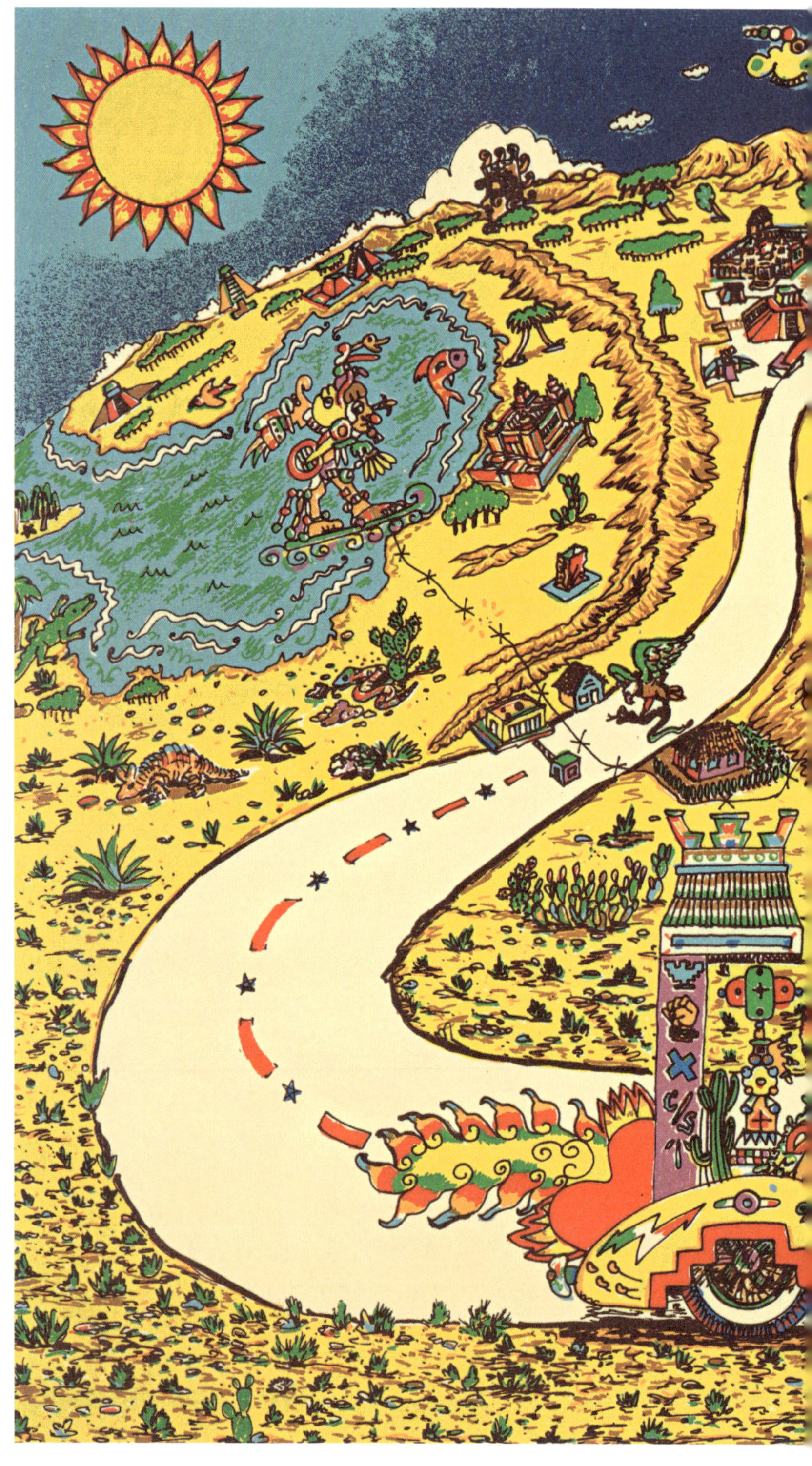

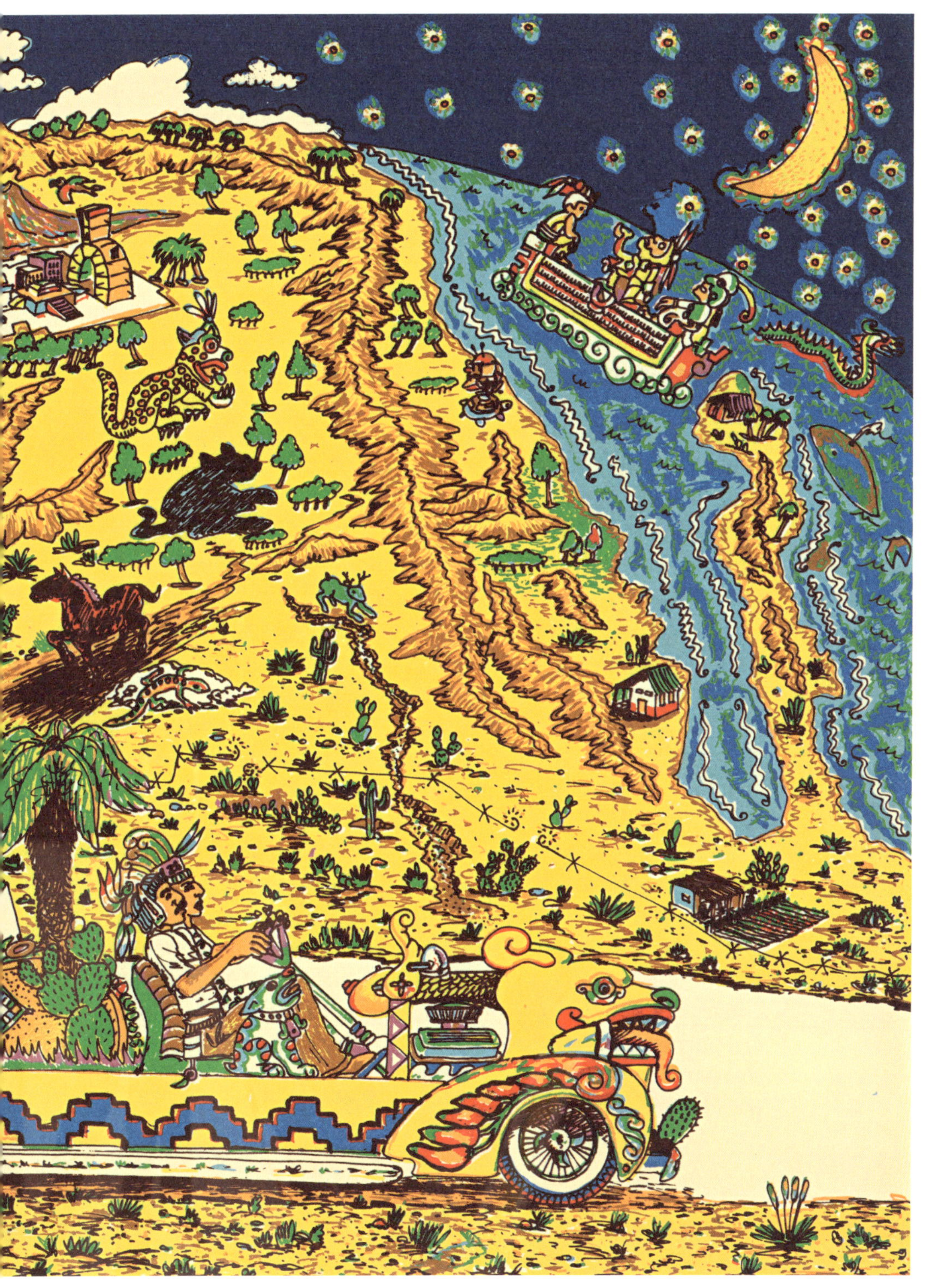

Gilbert "Magu" Luján, *Returning to Aztlán*, 1983
Fondation Collection Centre PasquArt

It depicts Mexico according to its current borders, the border region with the United States, the gulfs of Mexico and California, and a section of the Pacific Ocean. However, north and south are flipped—a deliberate move that visually and symbolically places Mexican culture above U.S. culture. *Returning to Aztlán* can therefore be interpreted as an allegory of "¡Arriba el pueblo!" ("Up With the People!"), the slogan that appeared regularly on the group's murals. It equally signifies Luján's rejection of the Mercator projection, a European- and U.S.-centric vision of the world. The piece can also be understood as a timeline, starting with Mesoamerican civilizations at the top, moving downward through the European invasions in the center (represented by the horse), and ending with 1970s Los Angeles at the bottom. Returning to Aztlán thus depicts a journey through space and time, suggesting a kind of cultural continuum between Native Americans, Mexicans and the Chicanos of Los Angeles. The vehicle for this journey, as depicted in the foreground, is a lowrider—a customized, lowered-suspension car strongly associated with Chicano culture. This car carries various symbols of Mexican culture: a palm tree, a cactus and oversized burritos and tacos. Graffitied on the vehicle is a raised fist, a symbol of the struggle for self-determination, while the man and woman driving the car reflect the artist's belief in gender equality. While *Returning to Aztlán* is undoubtedly a tribute to Luján's cultural heritage, it can also be interpreted as an artistic metaphor for the political movements of the 1960s and 1970s—an era of growing awareness of the systematic treatment of Chicanos as second-class citizens. In a lengthy text accompanying the work, the artist pointed to the fact that people who shared his ethnic identity were vastly overrepresented among soldiers sent to the front line in the Vietnam War. Luján concluded as follows: *"Returning to Aztlán* was indicative of a burgeoning concept of new ethnic cultural solidarity and determined political purpose. This artwork was intended to help educators to use this playful graphic tool and look into our history from los antepasados [the pioneers] unto the present."

1   The other group was Asco, which
consisted of Willie Herron, Harry
Gamboa Jr., Glugio "Gronk" Nicandro
and Patssi Valdez.

ARTISTS OF THE DONATION GLICKSMAN

Artists

John Alcorn
Peter Alexander
Carlos Almaraz
John Altoon
Carl Andre
Eleanor Antin
Shusaku Arakawa
Art & Language
Michael Asher
Alice Aycock
John Baldessari
Lewis Baltz
Derciq Bassani
Paul Beattie
Larry Bell
Billy Al Bengston
Wallace Berman
Joseph Beuys
Patrick Blackwell
Robert Branaman
Daniel Buren
Eugenia Butler
James Lee Byars
Alexander Calder
Rosemarie Castoro
Chermayeff & Geismar Associates
John Chamberlain
Judy Chicago
Bruce Conner
Ron Cooper
William N. Copley
Peter Davis
Guy de Cointet
William Crutchfield
Hugues Decointet
Marcel Duchamp
Jay DeFeo
Tom Eatherton
Jim Eller
Judy Fiskin
Llyn Foulkes
Dan Flavin
Sam Francis
Allen Ginsberg
Hal Glicksman
Joe Goode
Dan Graham
Robert Grosvenor
John Van Hamersveld
Newton Harrison
Phillip Hefferton
George Herms

Patrick Hogan
Hale H. Horton
Jasper Johns
Matsumi Mike Kanemitsu
Allan Kaprow
Edward Kienholz
On Kawara
Robert LaVigne
Sol LeWitt
Los Four
Gilbert Lujan
Kasimir Malevitch
Don Martin
Fred Mason
Michael McMillen
Richard Mock
Robert Morris
Bruno Munari
Clark Murray
Bruce Nauman
Edgar Negret
Richard Nonas
Maria Nordman
Claes Oldenburg
Eric Orr
Stuart Perkoff
Jeffrey Petrich
Shirley Pettibone
Robert Rauschenberg
Jane Reynolds
Frank Romero
James Rosenquist
Allen Ruppersberg
Edward Ruscha
Yuri Schwebler
Tony Scibella
Alexis Smith
Jack Smith
Robert Smithson
Jean St. Pierre
Lou Stovall
Marjorie Strider
Ben Talbert
Richard Tuttle
Cy Twombly
Kara Walker
Andy Warhol
Lawrence Weiner
Robert Whitman
Guy Williams
Hannah Wilke

Documentary Sets

KBCB

Exhibitions at Art Gallery UC Irvine:
Sketches and exhibition plans
Flyers
Posters
Catalogues and mock-ups

Exhibitions at Otis Art Institute Gallery:
Postcards
Sketches and exhibition plans
Flyers
Catalogues

Documents on Assemblagists:
Posters
Postcards
Catalogues

Documents on Pop Art:
Calendars
Posters
Catalogues

Documents on Light and Space:
Sketches and technical plans
Catalogues
Posters
Photographs

Documents on Chicano Art:
Posters
Calendar
Flyers

Documents on May 1968:
Posters

MAMCO

Artists of the Glicksman Donation, California: posters (c. 1960–1970), ephemera (c. 1960–1970), catalogues, among which two complete sets of ephemera by Allen Ruppersberg (1971–1985) and Guy de Cointet (1970–2015)

Books and catalogues, California, c. 1960 –1970 and Minimal art

Californian and international magazines, c. 1960–1970 (*Art & Langage, Avalanche, E.A.T. L.A.: Experiments in Art and Technology, La Mamelle, WET,* etc.)

Posters, Paris, May 68

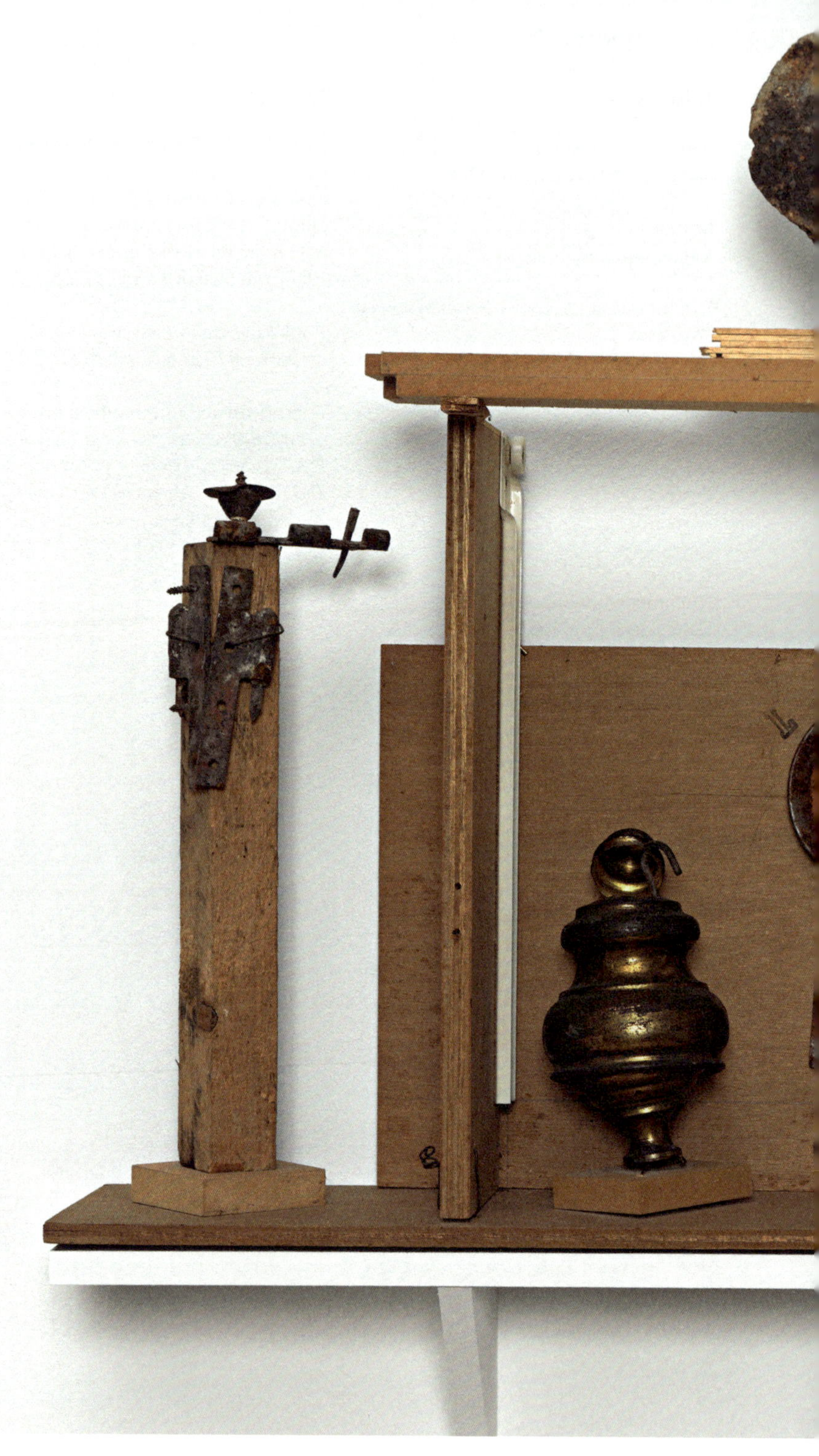

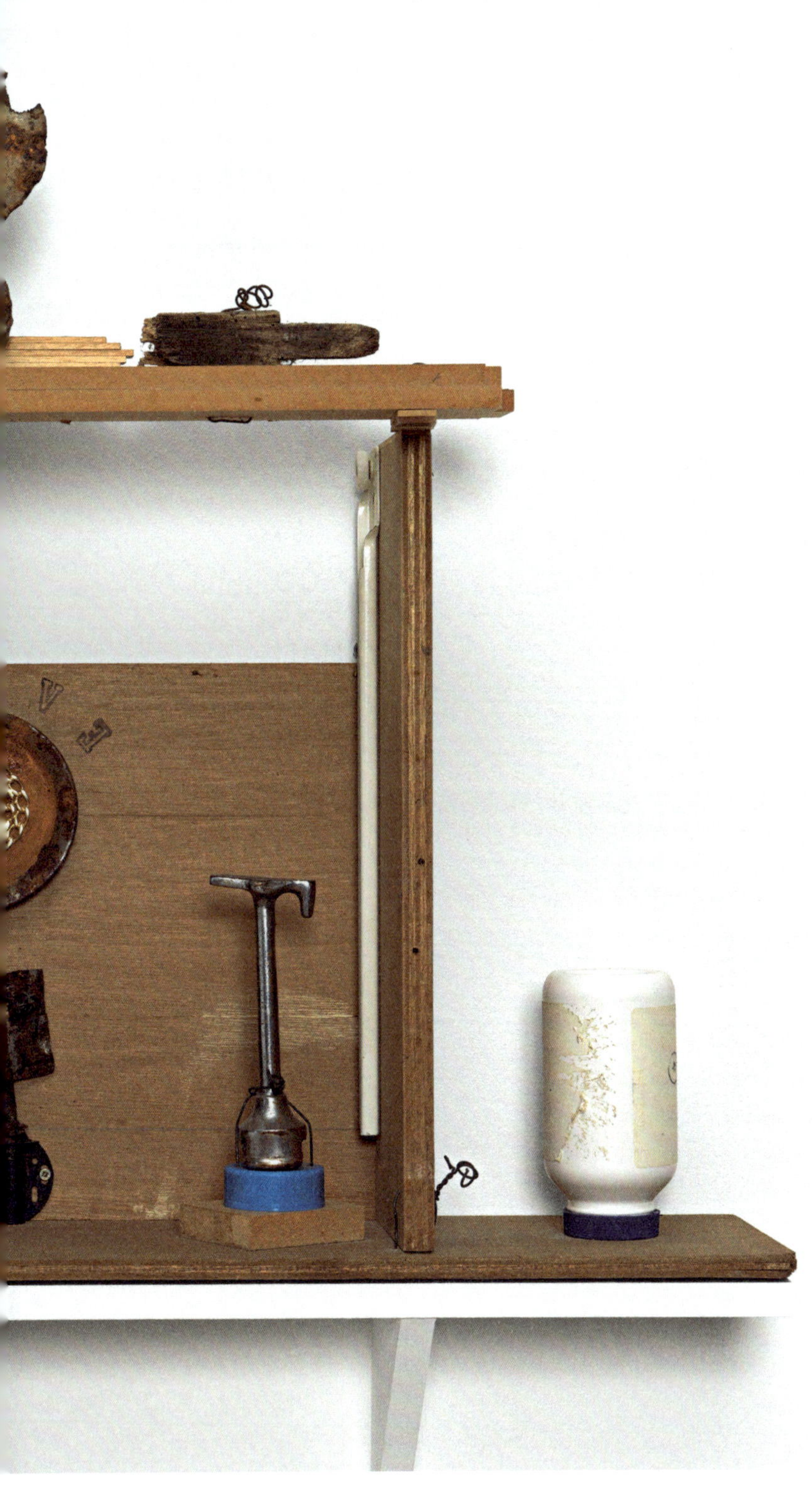

George Herms, *Ballet Box Light*, 2006
coll. MAMCO, don Mary Ann et Hal Glicksman

Impressum

Editorial Direction
  Lionel Bovier

Editorial Coordination
  Chloë Gouédard

Texts
  Paul Bernard
  Lionel Bovier
  Sophie Costes
  Julien Fronsacq
  Anne Giffon-Selle
  Gala Mayí-Miranda
  Jenna Paratte
  Laura Weber

Translations
  Christopher Scala

Cover Image
  Sigmund Fletcher (George Herms),
  Untitled, 1975

Design
  Gavillet&Cie/Devaud

Typefaces
  Apax, Practice (optimo.ch)

Prepress and Production
  Musumeci S.p.A, Quart (Aoste)

Printed and bound in Europe

Published with
ARTBOOK|D.A.P.
75 Brood Street
Suite 630
New York
NY 10004
www.artbook.com

ISBN 978-2-940656-12-7

Photo Credits
Annik Wetter: 2-7, 23, 24, 33, 46, 48,
  52-53, 58-59, 63, 64-65, 67, 68-69, 71,
  72-73, 79, 82-83, 92, 93, 95, 96, 101,
  107, 108, 132-133, 137
Lea Kunz: 8-13, 41, 45, 51, 54, 74, 117,
  123, 124-125
Getty Research Institute,
  Los Angeles: 28-29, 40, 80-81, 111,
  112-113
Julien Gremaud: 30, 49, 84, 118
Ilmari Kalkkinen: 87, 88-89

The series "MAMCO Collection"
is realized thanks to the support
of the Leenaards Foundation.

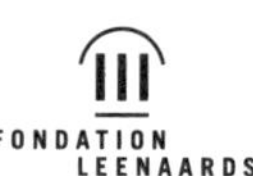

FONDATION
LEENAARDS

MAMCO
GENEVE

MAMCO Genève
10, rue des Vieux-Grenadiers
CH–1205 Genève
T +41 22 320 61 22
F +41 22 781 56 81
E info@mamco.ch

→
Bruce Conner, *Untitled*, 1970
coll. MAMCO, don Mary Ann
et Hal Glicksman

MAMCO opened in 1994 thanks to the perseverance of AMAM (Association for a Modern Art Museum, now Friends of MAMCO) and the generosity of eight patrons, who created the FONDATION MAMCO. Pooling together the support of its founders and, later, its co-founders, the foundation was the main source of funding and the sole governing body of the museum up until 2005, when it joined forces with the State and City of Geneva to create a public foundation, known as FONDAMCO.

MAMCO is overseen today by FONDAMCO, which is made up of FONDATION MAMCO, the Canton, and City of Geneva. FONDAMCO would like to thank all its partners, both public and private, and in particular: JTI, Fondation Leenaards, and Fondation VRM, as well as Fondation Bru, Fondation Coromandel, Fondation du Groupe Pictet, Fondation Jan Michalski, Fondation Lombard Odier, Fondation Philnor, Lenz & Staehelin, Mirabaud & Cie SA, Christie's, and Sotheby's.

FONDAMCO

Philippe Bertherat, President
Ronald Asmar, Vice-president
Anne Laure Bandle
Patrick Fuchs
Emmanuelle Maillard
Jérôme Massard
Carole Rigaut
Veronica Tracchia
Lada Umstätter

FONDATION MAMCO

Council
  Philippe Bertherat, President
  Luis Freitas de Oliveira, Vice-president
  Jean Marc Annicchiarico, Treasurer
  Karma Liess-Shakarchi, Secretary
  Charles Beer
  Jean-Pierre Greff
  Emmanuelle Maillard
  Shelby du Pasquier
  Simon Studer

Founders
  Claude Barbey
  Jean-Paul Croisier
  Pierre Darier
  André L'Huillier
  Philippe Nordmann
  Pierre Mirabaud
  Bernard Sabrier
  —as well as the Friends
  Association, represented by its
  President, Patrick Fuchs

Co-founders
  Anne-Shelton Aaron
    et Jean-Michel Aaron
  Antonie et Philippe Bertherat
  Marc Blondeau
  Maryse Bory
  Nicole Ghez de Castelnuovo
  Bénédict Hentsch
  Christina et Pierre de Labouchere
  Aimery Langlois-Meurinne
  Jean-Léonard de Meuron
  Nadine et Edmond de Rothschild
  Lily et Edmond Safra

Patrons
  Jean Marc Annicchiarico
  Antonie et Philippe Bertherat
  Association des Amis du MAMCO
  Verena et Rémy Best
  Marc Blondeau
  Bach-Nga Croisier
  Famille Darier
  Angela et Luis Freitas de Oliveira
  Christina de Labouchere
  Karma Liess-Shakarchi
  Emmanuelle Maillard
  Jean-Léonard de Meuron
  Pierre Mirabaud
  Jacqueline Nordmann
  Shelby du Pasquier
  Marine et Claude Robert
  Bernard Sabrier
  Fondation Safra, représentée
    par Samuel Elia
  Sophie Sallès de Meuron
  Simon Studer

TEAM

Lionel Bovier, Director

Museum Management and Development
  Valérie Mallet, Administrator
  Damien Grimm, Development
    Manager
  Chloë Gouédard, Library, Archives,
    and Museum Resources
  Julien Gremaud, Digital
    Communication
  Viviane Reybier, Press and
    Communication

Exhibitions and Collection
  Julien Fronsacq, Chief Curator
  Françoise Ninghetto, Honorary
    Curator
  Elisabeth Jobin, Curator
  Charlotte Schaer, Collection
    Curator
  Cyrille Maillot, Chief Exhibition
    Productions
  Filipe Dos Santos, Exhibition
    Productions and Collection
    Registrar
  Benoît Charron, Transport Registrar
  Pierre-Antoine Héritier and Caroline
    Dick, Associate Restorers
  Annik Wetter, Associate
    Photographer

Public and Education Services
  Yann Abrecht, Public Services
    Manager
Virginie Keller, Public Services
    Coordinator
Franco Osses Vidal, Public Services
    Coordinator
Charlotte Morel, Education Services
    Manager
Julie Cudet, Education Services
    Coordinator

Facility Management and Surveillance
  Antonio Magalhes, Chief of Facility
    Management
  Joana Gomes Da Silva, Facility
    Management
  Carlos Martins Fonseca, Surveillance

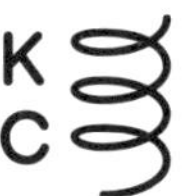
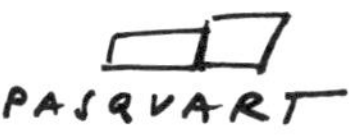

Kunsthaus Biel Centre d'art Bienne
Seevorstadt 71 Faubourg du Lac
CH-2502 Biel/Bienne
T + 41 32 322 55 86
E info@kbcb.ch | www.kbcb.ch

Paul Bernard, Director

Administration
  Manon Engel, Executive Assistant
    and Administrator Kunstverein
    Biel
  Gaby Siegenthaler, Accounting
    and Library

Exhibitions and Collection
  Laura Weber, Exhibition Manager
  Paolo Merico, Exhibition Production
  Gala Mayí-Miranda, Scientific
    Associate Collection and Library

Communication and Presse
  Delphine Peyronnet, Press

Art Education
  Lauranne Eyer, Art Education
    Manager
  Anna-Lena Rusch, Scientific
    Associate

Accueil du public et surveillance
  Gisela Meyer-Hänel, Reception
    Manager
  David Geiser, Reception
  Agnès Kucera, Surveillance
  Martine Bollo Mouchangou,
    Surveillance
  Ruben Monteiro, Surveillance

Cleaning
  Fatmire Qerimi, Cleaner
  Ramize Dzmailji, Agente d'entretien

Stiftung Kunsthaus-Sammlung
  PasquArt/Fondation Collection
  Centre d'art
  In 1991, a foundation was set up
  under the name Fondation
  Collection Centre d'art Pasquart,
  with the aim of building up a col-
  lection deposited at the Centre
  Pasquart and preserved according
  to the rules of art.

Council
  Heidi Schwab, President
  Ueli Schärrer, Vice-president
  Robert Spycher, Treasurer
  Jean-Pierre Bechtel
  Emanuela Tonasso
  Ruedi Vogt
  Michael Weissberg

Acquisitions Committee
  Paul Bernard
  Heidi Schwab
  Francisco Sierra
  Ueli Schärrer

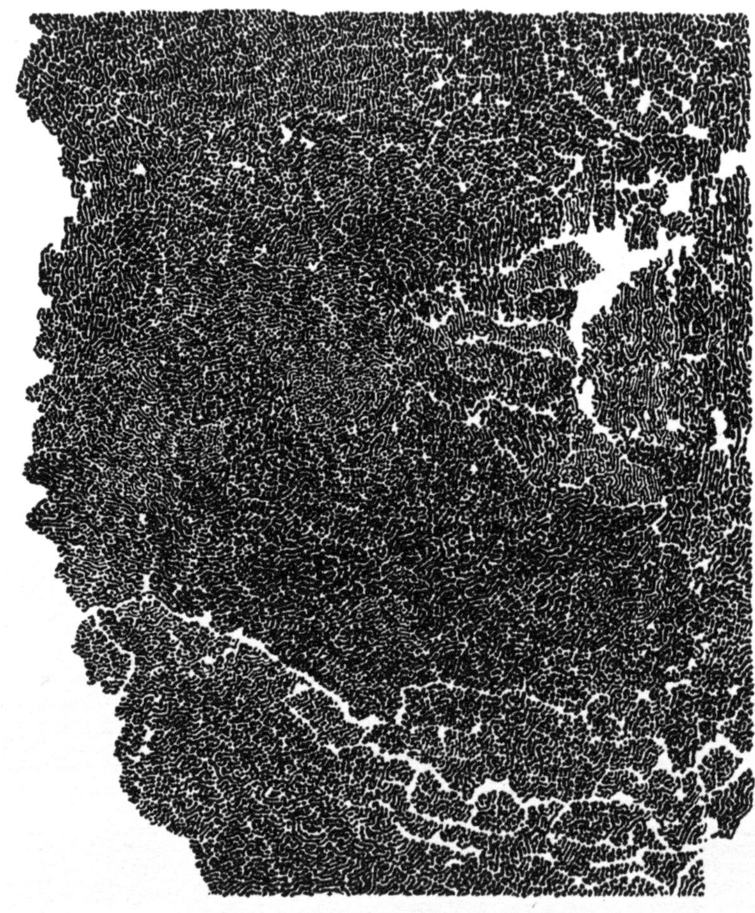

5/85
Conner